An
Awakening

An Awakening

Karen Baldwin

Faith in One

Faith In One, LLC
Murray, Utah

Published by Faith In One, LLC.

For more information please visit our web site at: www.karenbaldwin.net

Copyright © 2001 by Faith In One, LLC
Second Edition published in 2014

Cover illustration by Vadim Sadovski
Cover design by Lori Swapp
Interior design by Marny K. Parkin

ISBN-13: 978-0692207475

Printed in the United States of America

I would like to dedicate this book to my children,
Kimberly and Kevin
and to my granddaughter, McKenna,
and to God, for giving me a second chance;
A chance to awaken my mind
to the real purpose of life.
Without His love and guidance, this book
would not be possible.
I will forever be in your service.

Contents

Preface to the Second Edition

WHEN I FIRST WROTE "*AN AWAKENING*" IN 2001, I had never written anything before. I was just happy to be finished with it because writing it had taken me so long. I was learning how to type during the process of writing the book, plus living with my lung problems and all my physical duress! God helped me through it all.

I just wish it could have been done without so many mistakes and typos that first time! I have waited many years to be able to bring it back out for people to read because the miracles that have followed me for twenty years now have been *astounding* to say the least. This story needed to be told so that people could believe in God again.

It has been the most astounding thing that has ever happened to me! My life has changed dramatically and I am grateful for spirit in more ways than I could ever say. I hope you enjoy the read, there are many more to come . . .

Karen Baldwin
March 2014

Acknowledgments

FIRST, AND FOREMOST I WOULD LIKE TO THANK God for giving me the opportunity to experience this life and to change many of my wrongs. I would also like to thank my dearest friend, Kathy, and all of the people who have come to see me, attended my lectures, and those who have supported the very essence of who I am. I couldn't have done it without you.

I would like to extend a special, heartfelt 'thank you' to all of the doctors and nurses who have helped me to physically recover from the many sicknesses, accidents, and tragedies in my life. And my sincerest 'thank you' to Leslie, Chris, and Lee for their special contributions; and to Dan and Lori who provided technical support, editing, graphics, and layout, and the many hours of work they spent in an effort for this book to become a reality.

I would also like to thank my family for their turn-around of faith and support in my hours of need, and to my daughter, Kimberly, simply for being there and for having the ability to find patience with me.

May God bless you all, I will keep all of you in my heart forever . . .

Foreword

Kathy L. Foster

I WONDERED WHAT IT WAS ABOUT HER EYES. IT was as if I were looking at my own eyes, and yet, I wasn't. It went deeper than that. They were familiar, warm and loving. Was this the reflection of the sister I've always longed for but never had? I felt she knew my every thought; I knew I was safe with her. I felt sure she was my dearest friend and I was hers.

I first heard of Karen while I was attending a prayer circle. They talked about a lady in Salt Lake who had had a Near Death Experience that she lived to talk about. She had been invited to visit our circle and we all hoped that tonight would be the night she would show up. And she did! As I looked at her, her eyes embraced me with warmth; then I looked further and I saw she was on an oxygen machine. I wondered what had happened to her that was so severe that she needed oxygen. She was a small, petite woman about 5'2" and her hair was reddish-blonde and hung below her shoulders. She had beautiful, clear blue eyes and she spoke with a delightful southern accent. With a smile and a twinkle in her eyes, my heart melted and I knew that I had known her long before that evening.

I thought a lot about this gentle woman after meeting her, how shy and quiet she seemed, almost uncertain and afraid at times. I wanted to know her better. I wondered what made me feel like I needed to protect her and that somehow she needed me. I didn't know why I felt this way, but it was so strong that I called her a few days later. I was surprised she remembered everything about me. It wasn't until later that I found out that she knew things about most people—it didn't matter if she had met them or not. I asked her if she would be willing to speak of her experience to a group of my friends. She didn't hesitate for a minute, and said, "Sure honey, I'd love to." The meeting would take place a few weeks later. I was totally unaware that she had never spoken in front of a group before. This would be the beginning of her many, many group meetings telling others of her Near Death Experience.

We were all so eager and excited as we gathered tightly in her small living room. None of us knew what to expect. What happened that night changed my life forever. As Karen spoke, the energy of the room rose to one of perfect harmony. As she told her story, her hands would move rapidly with sign language. When I asked her when she learned to sign so well, she simply said, "I don't know, I just came back with it." That seemed to make her a little self-conscious and she tried to stop her hands from talking, but they wouldn't. I noticed that several times she tried to sit on her hands so they wouldn't move. But we all missed the beautiful, graceful movements. (In time she did stop signing.) We were captivated, watching and hearing this dear soul tell of her phenomenal experience. One minute we would all have tears rolling down our cheeks and the next minute her delightful sense of humor would show and we would all be laughing.

Very early in the evening we became aware that this was no ordinary person; there was something very unique about Karen. Here was this shy, quiet woman who spoke with such ease, grace and confidence. Speaking was definitely one of her gifts. And then, about half way through, we got the surprise of our lives, at least I did. We all had the feeling that there was someone else in the room, and every now and then she would look over our shoulders as if she was looking at someone a long way away. She would even talk to someone now and then, even though the rest of us couldn't see them. She would say things like, "I hear you," or "Okay I will." When I asked her if someone else was in the room she said, "Yes" and then everything opened up and she began to relay messages to some of us from those that she said had walked in with us (in spirit). As she spoke, we were all in tears again at the accuracy of her words from those that had come in with us. The proof was there in her words, we were beyond amazement. We couldn't even comprehend how she would know these things about people she had never heard of before.

As I tell people about Karen now, I tell them it's like she has one foot here and one foot on the other side. She definitely sees both sides very clearly. I thought I would never see anything that could top that night, but boy was I wrong! What was to come in the future was even more amazing. I soon realized that Karen's abilities went much further than any of us suspected. She spoke to us fluently in many other languages. I couldn't figure that out because in our visits she had told me that she hadn't even graduated from school. She had two children by the time she was eighteen, and by then she was alone tying to support her babies. I knew she hadn't completed any more schooling, and yet here she was fluently speaking the language of an old Indian tribal leader. Our evening went on for hours; we all knew it had to come to an end, and yet we couldn't leave. We asked her if she would speak to us again, and set up another meeting and another and another. So her public speaking had begun. The demand grew greater, and it seemed everyone wanted to hear Karen speak. I watched as her confidence grew; she couldn't understand why anyone would want to hear her talk. Karen is a very down-to-earth person, and that's one of the things people love so much about her.

When people began to call Karen to confirm that the things she had told them were true, she began to believe in herself more. It was hard for her at first, and she would ask me, "Am I really helpin' people, or am I losin' my mind?" I did everything in my power to help her believe in herself and her gifts, because I knew that if she was nuts so was I, because I believe strongly in her gifts and abilities. Karen had never heard of people like herself before. She had no knowledge about metaphysical ideas. Although she did notice that as she would touch people their pain would stop and healing would take place. But she said, "That just comes from Him," and she would point up.

Karen is just as normal and real as you and I. She has her ups and downs, her happy and sad times, and her sick and well times. Sometimes we would sit and cry and have what we called our "pity parties," and other times we really laughed at ourselves. As I looked at the scars on her body, and she told me the story of where they came from, I wondered how she lived through it all. Her physical body had been through a lot and the emotional scars were just as deep. She needed healing and she knew it. And as I watched her work through her stuff, the speed with which she could clear it away stunned me. What would take most people years upon years to release, she seemed to only take days—and I could see in her eyes when she was complete. There was always a new level of love, compassion, and peace and she was clear and new. She would learn and grow and move on from whatever would come up in her life. I really admire that about Karen, when I would express my amazement she would just point up and say, "They are helpin' me!"

As I look at Karen today, I see a somewhat different person with her cute new sassy haircut, which sparkles of highlights. She flashes her infectious smile and carries her oxygen tank wherever she goes. She is open, friendly, and outgoing. She's confident, with no fear of who she is or what she does. She has the outpouring of support of many thousands of people from all around the world—word of mouth traveled far! Her love for others is genuine, and her love for "Him" (as she points up) is what her life is all about. She's constantly telling me, "It's not me, it's Him."

Now she knows she hasn't lost her mind—thank heavens, and now I'm the one pointing up. She is humble and sees herself as no one special. She is the sister I never had, and I still ask, "What is it about those eyes?"

Introduction

Karen Baldwin

THESE WORDS AREN'T WHAT YOU ARE PROBably used to reading, but they are all mine. Many of the friends that I have made over the last few years have asked me to put together my experiences so that others could read them. It was very hard for me to write this book. This isn't just a story, it's my life. I never finished school; in fact, the last grade I completed was the sixth grade. This book was typed with two fingers and the grace of God.

Since my accident in September of 1994, my life has drastically changed. It has taken a toll on my family and what it's done to me . . . well, that's why I'm writing this book. I feel like I've been living in a different world altogether. Since I came back, nothing has been the same for me at all. My life now is 'a twist to a different wrench,' as I call it.

As I look back at it all now, the near death experience helped me to grow in many ways, and I'm thankful; but it wasn't easy, no matter how you look at it. I think that some fools have had the misconception that I slid through it all like a hot knife through butter—not even. I wish it had been that simple. I wasn't sure who the real Karen was anymore. All the things I had learned in my life had suddenly taken on a different meaning. I was very frightened in the beginning with all the thoughts that were flowing through my mind. Nothing in my life seemed to make any sense to me at all. To this day I still have 'my Kodak moments,' as I call them. Sometimes all it takes is just an odor, something in the air that I don't expect to smell, and it takes me rushing back to that morning. That moment that changed me from who I was to who I am.

I begin to get sweaty palms, I feel jittery inside my stomach. It isn't fear, it's only my physical body reacting to something that my mind recalls—the intense pain as if I had been swallowed up by a ball of fire, and I begin to relive the experience all over again, like it happened yesterday. My mind starts to swim with all that I can remember from being on the other side. I get swept away in the turbulence like a wind storm and it still rattles my cage. On the one hand, I'm downright knocked off my feet to think that this really happened to me; and on the other, I'm in awe at how it all works. I have tried so very hard to understand it all. In the beginning nothing made sense. Bits and pieces of memory crowded my mind of being there and the Guardian. So many different things happened to me that day. I couldn't for the life of me tell you where to start with it all. I have cried to God to help me, to please just take me back to that beautiful place that the Guardian and I were at, but it just hasn't happened yet.

My poor family didn't know how to help me. At that time in my life, *I* didn't know how to help me. I didn't know how to help myself, or even where to begin. I had never heard of this type of thing before, so I had no clue as to what was really going on inside of me. My family thought that I had "went off the deep end," if you know what I mean. How could they possibly help me with something that they couldn't understand? I'd seen things they couldn't see and heard things they couldn't hear. If this sounds confusing, I simply say, "Welcome to my world." None of us were ready for what happened to me that morning, or what would follow. The accident at the dry cleaners changed me and my life—including my family—and nothing has been the same since.

The following pages contain real life episodes from my life, but I have changed the names of the people included to preserve their right to privacy.

My Journey Home

I MOVED TO SALT LAKE CITY IN MARCH, 1993. That August, I went to work for some people who had been in the dry cleaning business for many years. Their children were in the process of taking over the business because their parents were going to retire.

There were many new chemicals that we were told were safe to use. Some would turn the worst stain white again and still protect the garment. Barbara was in her early twenties and had worked for this family for about five years. She had just been given the title of acting supervisor at this store, but she was as new to some of these chemicals as I was.

I remember the day we first started working with one particular chemical called a *Stripper*. It was an industrial-strength bleach that came in a white powder form. We would sprinkle the powder on the garment, then slightly dampen the spot with a couple of drops of water to start the action of the powder. Then we would tap on the garment with a flat-head brush, working the fabric. With a high-powered steam gun, we would then try to flush out the chemical along with the spot on the garment, all the while holding down the vacuum peddle built into the table that we were spotting on with our foot. This vacuum helped to pull away the vapors that would come up from the chemicals we were using.

It was quite a process to perform. If you didn't use the steam gun in the right way, you could either burn your fingers real bad or put a hole in the garment so we had to be careful. The *Stripper* had a different odor than that of ordinary household bleach; it had a very pungent smell and it would leave a metallic taste in my mouth for hours after I had used it.

The first day we used the *Stripper*, there was an incident with a white sweater. We were in the process of trying to remove a spot on the front of a garment. As Barbara and I were working with the sweater, that cotton-pickin' sweater started to dissolve right before our eyes! We both gasped and looked at each other in disbelief as to what was taking place—it was literally disappearing! I grabbed that sucker and did the fifty-yard dash, running to the back of the building where the bathroom was, that was the only sink we had. I put the sweater in the sink and started flushing it with water trying to stop the action of the chemical, but it was too late. There in my hands was a sweater with a hole the size of a golf ball. The chemical had eaten its way right through that darn sweater. It was totally amazing how fast it all happened. Our boss Tim ended up having to replace the garment. From then on we were very careful about how we used that particular chemical.

Not long after that incident, the industrial company introduced us to another new chemical. I'll call it *"Devour,"* because that is just what it would do. The purpose of this chemical was to eat protein. I had a very negative physical reaction the first time I had contact with it, and I wasn't even using it at the time. I was about eight feet away, at my station pressing clothes, and Barbara was using the chemical. She must not have had her foot on the vacuum pedal that helps to draw off the odors, because the vapors were being blown away from her by the high-powered steam gun—but it was directing most all of the chemical toward my pressing table instead of pulling them into the vacuum.

At the time, there was no way that she could have known what was gonna happen. I started feeling like someone was sitting in the middle of my chest. At first I just tried kicking the feeling off, but I just wasn't breathing good at all; I didn't know what was going on. I started coughing and gasping for air. The odor that filled the room was choking me right down. My lungs were burning like crazy the more I tried to breathe in. I began to realize it was the fumes that were around me that were making me feel worse. The chemical that Barbara was using was releasing a toxic vapor that was knocking me off my feet. My nose started swelling up on the inside. I could only breathe through my mouth, and even that wasn't enough air, my throat burned so bad. I finally took off outside, I knew I needed some fresh air, fast!

Tim was upstairs in his office. He was told that something was terribly wrong with me. There were others working there that day that were affected as well, but not as bad—they were in other parts of the building, not in direct contact, as I had been. After ten or fifteen minutes of fresh air, I thought that I would be okay. I tried to go back inside, but the chemical vapors took its toll on my lungs. My whole chest felt like it was going to cave in. The smell literally would not let me back inside the building. The whole ordeal left me pretty shook up and I had to go home for the rest of the day.

Tim posted a note that this chemical was not to be used in my presence anymore by anyone. However, that chemical was used around me without my knowledge one more time, and the same thing happened again. For some reason, Barbara thought that it would be all right if she used a little bit of the chemical, that a small amount probably wouldn't bother me. But as soon as she began to use the chemical, the same doggoned thing happened to me again.

I was upset that this darn stuff had been used around me again, and gave Tim notice that I was gonna have to quit my job. He wasn't too happy about that, and I guess Barbara didn't think that I would quit, but I was ready to do just that. I should have left right then and there. Tim asked me to give him a couple of days to see what changes he could make. I agreed because I knew that if I left at that time he would have been in deep doo-doo with all the clothes that were needing to be pressed. There was a lot of work to be done and no one else to do it.

I took a lot of pride in doing a good job. At times, my co-workers and I would have races to see who could press the most clothes in the shortest amount of time, and it helped to make the time pass. Tim didn't want to lose me, so a couple of days later I was sent to one of his other stores, which was a Laundromat and Dry Cleaners. He asked me if this would be all right and informed me that I would be the only one that would work with the chemicals while I was on my shift, so I would know what was being used and shouldn't have any problems. I went ahead and agreed to his offer to change to the other store.

Tim also asked if I would like to learn more about the process of spotting with chemicals. Even though I had already been using some of these chemicals, I had no clue at the time as to how they worked, so I agreed to go to a two-hour seminar to learn more about them. There I was shown how to use some of the different chemicals on all types of cloth. I accepted the job as "The Spotter" and I would still press clothes as well. After a while many customers would bring their belongings in and specifically ask for me to take care of their clothes. I guess I must have been doing something right.

There were three of us who worked at the new store. Dan and Susan were in their twenties, and I felt like a mom to everyone because I was forty-five at the time. I had shared with Susan about how strange I would feel some days after working. I felt as though ants were crawling all over my back. I asked her if she had ever felt like that. She said that she would sometimes get real headachy or dizzy. There was not one exhaust fan in the whole dad-gum building, so we would open up the doors to air the building out. At times the fumes were so pungent even the patrons of the Laundromat would remark of headaches and burning eyes, or they would just start coughing and walk outside. Many times I was asked if we had any aspirin to treat headaches.

This was an old building with old machinery. There were a lot of leaks in the small room where the dry cleaning machine was. *Perkclorethyline* (we called it *Perk*, for short), the dry cleaning chemical, constantly dripped onto the floor. Dan or I would clean out the lint baskets to prevent it from overflowing and leaking so much. The room was maybe six feet long and maybe three feet wide, if it was even that big. The air was always stagnate behind the dry cleaning machine. There were no air vents in the room that I ever saw. The repair men that had to go inside this room when the dry cleaning machine was broken were always complaining of the tight quarters. They were always bumping their elbows or their heads inside of this room.

The boiler room was just as bad. There were so many rusty pipes, it was amazing the water would run clear. But our work needed to be done, so we just made the best of it.

One morning in September, 1994, I woke up about 2:30 in the morning, way too early to go to work, but that didn't make any sense to me. It wasn't pay day, and I had no reason to be up early. But I kicked off the feeling and just decided to go on into work and put all that enthusiasm to good use.

I had the keys to the building, so I let myself in. It was 4:59 when I punched in that morning. As I walked through the Laundromat, I could smell all the stale odors that were mixed together. It was a pungent smell that still lingered inside the building from the day before, but it seemed different somehow. All the chemicals had a mustiness—it was thick and seemed to be just hanging in the air.

Then I began to notice something different in my sinuses. There was a nasty smell that seemed to get stronger the closer I got to the back of the building. I walked inside the boiler room and turned on a couple of the lights. We had been having trouble with it building up enough pressure to run the irons and the other machinery. I had to turn the boiler on so it could build up steam. I crossed my fingers that the blessed thing would work right today. I figured as soon as the boiler was up to snuff, I could start pressing all the clothes that were hanging on the line waiting for me. It looked as though I had a full day of pressing clothes in front of me from the way the line was packed.

I had brought my brother's chef whites with me that morning to try and get some of the stains out. I knew regular bleach couldn't touch most of the food stains, and I wanted him to look his best so he could make a good impression on his new boss. I was thinking that if I made a strong batch of the chemical solution, then I could soak his whites while I was busy doing my other work. I always kept my soak bucket in the back where the boiler room was. My brother's clothes could be soaking for several hours before I had to run them through the washer, then they should look real nice. Yup, that sounded like a plan to me.

So I headed to the back of the building and went to the smaller room where the dry cleaning machine was. I passed by my working station. As I walked by my pressing table I noticed a bunch of stinking rags that were laying all around it. "Great, just great," I said. I sure wasn't a happy camper at this point. I was perturbed to think that whoever had used my area didn't even clean it up! I had always tried to leave things clean and tidy because we were in the public eye and the customers could see everything behind the counter. I just shook my head in disbelief.

As I walked by the spotting table, I saw two empty containers of *Devour* still sitting there. This was the chemical that had caused me so much trouble. My stomach wrenched at the thought of what had happened to me the day Barbara had used it. I remembered how bad it had made me feel and how sick I got from breathing this nasty stuff. It had caused me so much physical pain, not to mention the fact of the upset that followed shortly after when I told my boss that I would have to quit my job.

I decided that Julie must have been here over the weekend. She was the new Floating Manager and she was the only one that had keys to all the stores to my knowledge. She had to have been the one using this darn stuff. I threw the empty containers into the trash can, wiping my hands on the towel that lay on the table. "Yuck," I said out loud. I didn't like the way it made me feel inside—just holding the containers in my hands gave me the heebie-geebies.

I walked back to the smaller room where the dry cleaning machine was. It was a mess as well. The lint baskets were full from the cleaning that had been done over the weekend. No one had bothered to empty the lint baskets. *Perk* (the dry cleaning solution) was dripping onto the floor and there was a large area of the cement floor that was wet from the overflow. "Grrrreat!" I thought to myself, "That's all I needed this mornin' is to have to clean this dang mess up as well. OSHA would have a field day with this one if they saw it."

The fumes were horrible. It was taking my breath away, just walking inside the room. I grabbed the protective face mask that was up on the shelf and I put it on quickly. I remembered telling Dan what I thought the first time I tired the face mask on. We laughed 'cause I told him I thought it made me look like a red headed fly. I smiled at this thought. It never bothered me makin' people laugh even if it was me they were laughing at. I also put on the thick black rubber gloves that almost reached my elbows and were five times larger than my hands. That was all I had for my protection. *Perk* is highly toxic and can burn your skin if it touches it very long. It also can enter the pores of your skin, causing physical harm and cancer.

The fumes seemed to be getting worse. It was as if the darn mask wasn't working right. I pulled the straps on the face mask tighter on my head, thinking that this would help to keep the vapors out. I felt the rubber tightening against my cheeks, although it didn't seem to make a difference. I could still smell the vapors real bad, so I hurried to try and finish cleaning up the mess. I thought maybe the filters that were in the two face pockets weren't good anymore. Maybe they needed to be replaced because the smell was still so strong. I started to get lightheaded. I needed to hurry up and get the heck out of there.

I finished cleaning out the lint baskets and then went and got the rags that were left at my pressing table. I used them to clean up the *Perk* that was on the floor. I put the rags inside the machine so that the smell and chemicals could be recycled again. The residue that was left on the floor would have to air dry. I left the room and took off my face mask and gloves and laid them on the shelf. I opened the side door and stepped outside for a little bit, I needed some fresh air after all that. I started feeling a lot better now with that darn mask off my face and the mess cleaned up.

It was still a little dark and quiet outside. The air felt cool and it smelled good as I stood there for a minute just talking in the stillness of the city. After a few minutes I figured that I ought to get back to work. I was burning daylight and I needed to get my butt in gear, there was a lot of work to get done today. I stepped back inside the building closing the door behind me. The air inside was just as thick as it had been before. The only fan in this cotton picking place was the swamp cooler. There were no exhaust fans anywhere. I had brought a little 12 inch fan from home for my personal use so it made it more comfortable when I was pressing clothes, but there was no way of blowing the smell out of the building.

I reached for the chemical on the spotting table that I needed to start my bleach batch. As I looked down at the empty plastic containers in the trash can, I wondered why in the heck Julie had used the *Devour*, and why here, of all places. "Why didn't she go to one of the other stores?" I thought. It just didn't make any sense to me at all.

By now it was about 5:20 a.m. or so, but no later than 5:30. I headed toward the boiler room to get my five-gallon white bucket. I knew that I should have plenty of steam and hot water by now. I had been using the same white five-gallon bucket to do my bleaching in for quite some time. When I walked back into the boiler room

I saw the bucket there on floor by the sink. I glanced inside, it appeared to be empty. I put the bucket inside the sink and poured the powdery chemical into the bucket. I looked inside and thought, "Maybe I'll add just a little bit more. These are some really bad food stains on my brother's white clothes." I knew it was going to take a miracle to get them clean. Then I turned on the hot water. The water hit the chemical, and what happened next I wasn't prepared for at all.

I had been breathing normally, and all of a sudden I felt like I was inhaling fire. I grabbed a hold of the side of the sink so I wouldn't fall. I had closed my eyes because the pain was so intense, and fumbled frantically, trying to feel for the faucet to turn the water off. More and more steam kept coming up. I couldn't hold my breath because I was trying so hard to keep breathing, it was so overwhelming for me. My eyes were closed and I was choking and gasping for air, air that just didn't seem to be there. I was suffocating. I knew I was in deep trouble. My lungs felt as though they were on fire. I remember trying to scream as I gasped for air with my hands up to my face.

"SWEET JESUS HELP ME! OH MY GOD PLEASE MAKE IT STOP!" were my thoughts!

All of a sudden everything went very still. I heard a ringing sound in my ears and there was a buzzing inside of me somewhere and I could hear a high pitched tone of some kind. Then there was a loud rushing sound that went through my head but I felt no pain—I was so surprised at how peaceful I seemed to feel.

I thought to myself, "Man that was close! thank God, I'm okay!"

Then I lowered my hands from my face. I could not for the life of me understand what I was looking at right then. The first things that I saw were my hands. I felt they were mine, *but they were different*. I was looking at them and it was as if they were *translucent gold threads*, not at all what I was used to looking at. They were totally different, yet I knew these were *my hands*. They had a beautiful look about them. That's when I noticed that *I could see right through them.*

"How can this be?" I thought. I remember touching myself with both hands. "I can feel me," I was thinking, "This *is* me, but how can this be?" That's when I noticed it was pitch black all around me. Just black, as if I were inside of a void.

My mind raced with questions, "Where is the boiler room? Where am I at?" I wasn't frightened, I just didn't understand what was going on. I looked back at my hands, and then I noticed *"her"* laying on the floor below me.

I felt as though I was suspended several feet above the ground, and there below me was this little lady laying in a fetal position. I knew that she was dead; there was no life inside of her. All of her physical functions had stopped working. She was laying in her own urine and waste, I could see that.

I thought, "What in the world has happened here?" I felt confused at first; I really didn't know what was going on. Her body seemed to be so empty, so fragile and so small. I felt that it really wasn't necessary to do any-thing for her. I was not emotionally linked to this body, and yet as I looked closer that's when it hit me—*the lady was me!* I never knew that I looked so skinny. I always thought that I was much bigger than what I appeared to be. I had always seen myself as being much stronger, with an attitude, ya know. I always thought of myself as a 'tuffy'—at least I thought I was.

Then I began to feel a pulling sensation coming from behind me. Like a magnet would feel, being drawn to it. I looked, and saw the most beautiful, radiant light, and I wanted to get closer to it. I either started moving toward it or it moved toward me, I don't know which was first. I moved away from the body that was on the floor. I remember looking into the light, and then I turned back to look at the body once more. All of a sudden I thought to myself, "I'm out of here!" I never felt se free as I did at that moment.

I was moving very, very fast. Now the darkness had turned into the most beautiful colors that were all around me. My surroundings were completely different. I was no longer in the boiler room. The colors changed in front of me like a rainbow, as if I were inside of a prism of soft blues, grays, and turquoise colors. They swirled all around me as if I were in a fog or mist of some kind. The sensation felt wonderfully cool to me. I felt safe and secure. There was some kind of a vibration that I could feel.

Off in the distance I could hear some kind of music. It was as if it were coming out of a hallway or some other place that had depth to it, somewhere far away. The sound was incredibly beautiful, it was like a choir was singing somewhere. I could only hear the tune; I never heard voices, just the music. The sound was so soft and tranquil; so comforting to hear. I felt a total peace coming over me that was so profound. I was surrounded by the light and

I felt completely calm. There was a mist-like atmosphere around me and I felt I was no longer on Earth.

That's when I noticed a figure inside of the mist coming into my view. As it got closer I recognized my son. He lived in California! I could see him sitting at a table. He was talking to a buddy of his about some kind of tree work that needed to be taken care of. They were both tree trimmers, and I could actually hear them talking. I was amazed at what I was seeing. But he couldn't see me. He didn't even know I was there. I thought to myself, "The things that he really needed to know are hidden deep down inside of him, but I couldn't communicate with him." I wanted to let him know so bad.

Then the hues and blues seemed to swirl around me as if I were in the middle of a beautiful prism again. I felt as if I where speeding along in this soft color, in my own space of some kind. Then it got real light. In the mist I could see another figure. Closer and closer I got until I could see my daughter. She was at her job in Salt Lake City. She worked for a doctor at the time, and there she was sitting at her desk. She was talking to someone on the phone pertaining to a delinquent bill. This person was giving my daughter a headache. I could feel the tension that was mounting inside of her. I wanted so much to change her frustration, but I couldn't touch her at all. I wanted to tell her that everything would be okay, but I couldn't. Then as swiftly as I had arrived, I left.

The mist returned and so did the colors of blues and hues. Now I could see my granddaughter. This precious little darling was at the child daycare center. I thought, "How sad, she will never know how very much I really love her." I wanted to let her know how wonderful I thought she was. What a blessing she had been for my daughter. Then suddenly I was moving away again through the blues and the hues. The light was penetrating my very existence, warming the center of who I was and reminding me how much I was loved by all my family.

"That's funny," I thought to myself, "I still feel like me." I felt at the moment so much joy and harmony with everything that was around me. I was as if I were truly part of every living thing that I ever touched or saw.

I began to move faster and faster. I felt as though I was moving in an upward direction. I saw these real bright lights rushing past me. Some were moving much faster than I was, while others seemed to float effortlessly, enjoying their new-found freedom and direction. They were shaped in the figure of a ball and they glowed as if they had a light inside of them. I knew we were all going to the same place; how I knew that, I don't really know, but I did. I saw what appeared to be different colors that had a great depth to them.

Further and further I traveled at a high rate of speed. It was as if I was going through a galaxy or universe of some kind, it was so vast. Faster and faster I moved. In the distance I could see what appeared to be a star creating itself, as if in a dimension all of its own; so vibrant were the colors. You could see all the gases coming from inside its own creation; it was magnificent. I had never seen such an extraordinary thing as this before. It was as if it had a clear energy field that surrounded it. I was somehow aware of this and everything else that was around me at that precise moment.

I seemed to be floating aimlessly, now at a much slower rate of speed. In front of me appeared the most beautiful landscape, reaching out to points that seemed to separate into different dimensions, as if on different levels, but not levels of good or bad. They were levels of understanding. Deep knowledge that was supreme for all that was there. Such a splendor! When I was alive I never thought that I could have such a reward as this, not with the way I had chosen to live my life.

Suddenly I realized that instead of getting two-blades-of-grass in the lower-forty, I had made it to a much better place than I could have ever imagined. I knew God had created all of this. I seemed to flow effortlessly across the land. Everything was so warm with color and full of life. Now my inner being was very aware of where I was at. There were ponds and rivers that ran into each other. The water looked much different than what I was accustomed to seeing—it was as if the colors reflected off of everything; the water was so incredibly clear. It didn't look like normal water to me, it was so pure; it shimmered with a life force that you could feel, that's the only way I know how to describe it. The life force was in everything that I could see and life was in all that I saw. This was indeed the most incredible sight.

Scattered here and there I could see small groups of people walking and talkin; to one another. As I moved slowly by them our eyes met. They acknowledged me with a smile, as if they knew me. They were dressed in light robes of some kind. Most all of the people were dressed alike with a few exceptions. Some of the people that I saw in the distance had light gray spots on their robes. I felt that they were in a process of healing old wounds from the lives they had lived on Earth.

At that time I looked at my hands, thinking to myself, *"I must be dead. I must have died there on the floor!"* I was looking at this beautiful flesh that appeared to be my hands. I knew it was still me, the real me, "But how?" I gazed at this miracle that had taken place.

As the moments passed, I realized that I seemed to have all of my normal abilities, yet I knew I was *different*. I could move quickly and go wherever I wanted to with just a thought. I felt light and there was no weight to me. I simply had to let my thoughts generate and I was that thought in mind. This was absolutely amazing to me, I felt so overwhelmed and excited.

"How beautiful a place to be and to share it with all that was around me; how lucky I am to be here in this peaceful place with such splendor," I thought. I wanted to continue to have this wonderful feeling and never let it stop. The area and all the colors were so intense. This place was like nothing I had ever seen before; and yet I knew this was home, my place to be.

There were meadows and paths coming from many different directions all leading into the center of a city. I was looking at rolling hills that were in the distance, although they seemed to be in another dimension of some kind. I knew as I looked upon the city that each of the buildings were packed full of knowledge about Earth and other places in our universe. The trees seemed as if they had the breath of life in them, soft and flowing. The leaves were like millions of tiny voices softly saying they were delighted to see me. I could feel them loving me and telling me they were glad I was home. Their beauty was so incredible. The light seemed to reflect their colors at every angle off of the leaves as if they had been sprinkled with dewdrops. The flowers were like none that I had ever seen; they glowed with colors that had such depth to them, such detail in each petal as if they had been hand-painted. They covered the ground of a wonderful large meadow. They were filled with a pulsating life force that moved inside of them. There were millions of them all over the ground; the color reminded me of a never-ending rainbow laying across a field like a blanket, it was endless.

As I gazed at all that surrounded me I didn't want to miss seeing anything. I noticed a bridge some distance away from me. That's when I saw HIM standing on the other side of the bridge. He stood out from everyone else. He was so majestic and yet appeared to be soft; as if he were radiating love and serenity from deep inside of Him. He glowed as though light was coming from inside of his frame. His face was not like anyone I had ever seen before. His magnificence was one that I recognized in my heart. As strong as he appeared to be, He was also gentle and very loving. To describe Him is difficult. I knew He knew me. Our thoughts became one at that moment and I asked Him, "Did I die? 'Cause if I did, I ain't going back, okay?"

"Are you sure?" I felt His response as our thoughts seemed to intertwine with each other. I felt a burst of love and peace and inner bliss that I had never known before. *"There has been an accident, but you need not be here,"* was what I heard in my mind. He said nothing to me with a voice, only by telepathic means did I ever hear anything from Him.

I glanced down at the water's edge below the bridge. I wanted a drink awfully bad. I asked if I could have a drink of the water. There was no reply. I looked at Him, He was so breathtaking and magnificent. He (the Guardian as I refer to Him) was possibly ten or twelve feet tall. He was radiant, and all I could feel was His perfection, His peacefulness, and His love for me. He was standing by what appeared to be an emerald rock. As I drew closer to the Guardian, I noticed that the emerald had beautiful edges, as if I were looking at a finely cut crystal or diamond. I could see light working its way through it. It was very, very large. I was still feeling thirsty at this point. Again I asked the Guardian if I could get a drink of water out of the creek. He simply gestured toward the rock as if He wanted me to look at it.

I moved closer, and saw the emerald changing deep from within. As I looked closer, I noticed it had taken on a different look. Something was pulling me until I was infused in its beauty. It swirled with the luster of a soft pinkish-blue color that was warm and comforting to me, drawing me deeper into it with just a glance. I could feel something around me as if there was a substance of fluid. Suddenly I could hear my mother's voice. It was as if I were watching television—I could see both of my parents. Mama was saying, "Johnny, I've got something to tell ya."

He let out a sigh and hung his head low and said, "Don't tell me the toilet is messed up again."

"No . . . ," she replied, "We're gonna have a baby!"

At that point was when I realized I could feel myself in my mother's womb as she talked to Daddy. I had seen and felt how much my mother was looking forward to my birth. My life review began at that point moving very, very fast. I saw my whole life working itself out in front of me.

Most all of this was overwhelming for me. *I was viewing my life.* I could feel all of the emotions of everyone I could see; I was watching it all, and yet there was no judgment being made by anyone. I was purely a spectator as the events of my life began to play out in front of me. I saw where a male family member had assaulted me at the age of three. After finding this out Mama and Daddy talked with my Gamma about it. They thought that it would be best that the family member be sent away. No one wanted to tell the police what had happened. They were afraid the police would lock him up for the rest of his life. They thought that I would be all right and that he wouldn't hurt anyone else. That had not been his intention to begin with, and physically I was okay. My family had hoped that I had been young enough that I would not have memory of the assault. He didn't know what he had done to me was wrong 'cause he was of a simple mind—a young boy in a man's body who did not know right from wrong. The emotion that I felt was forgiveness and compassion for him and my parents.

Many of the things that I saw gave me a better understanding as to why my life had taken the course it had. At that moment, for the first time, I was seeing Mama and Daddy for the ordinary people that they were. I understood them individually. I felt compassion for them both. Without judgment I continued viewing my life from all different directions.

As I got older I had made many mistakes, many times at the cost of others feelings, and I had not cared at the time. My mind was impressed with these thoughts from the Guardian, *"If you just add love, you will feel love."* This was showing me so much. At that point I really could understand what had happened to me and to my family. I saw who I was . . . and what I had become.

As it all worked out in front of me, I was able to understand things at a much deeper and more compassionate level. I understood all of the feelings that had been so jumbled up inside of me for so many years. I wanted to forgive everyone that had ever hurt me. I felt so much compassion for my parents. I could feel the heaviness of regret that they held in their hearts. I could feel it—the hell they put themselves through. They never could forget or forgive themselves for what had happened to me. They always blamed each other for it and it consumed them. It ruined their lives and had bruised mine. Their marriage of fifteen years was destroyed, and their love for each other was lost in the pain of it all. I saw the true importance of forgiveness and unconditional love that should have been there that unfortunately dissipated because of this tragedy. I could see the devastation and all the grief that it had caused them and myself as a child. My thought was, "Oh God please forgive them. All those years that were covered up in such pain."

As quickly as that time frame had come for me to view, now it was gone and more of my life was laid out for me to examine in whatever way I wanted to. Out of my own fear, *I saw where it had been my choice not to change many of the things that I could have in my life. I had not learned how to love myself.* I saw where I had a big lack of trust, even for those that genuinely cared for me. Some of the people I had chosen to take into confidence had not been good influences for me. I had picked up anger and stubbornness trying to physically fight my way throughout most of my life. I saw how hurt and foolish I had been—instead of seeing the deeper purpose of my life and what I could have done with it. I saw how my life had consumed me.

I saw, too, that many of the choices that I had made in my life had not been good, and the results of many of them would carry on into my children's lives. The effect on my daughter and son would show in many different ways. Because of me. I could see the damage that I had caused, and I was very ashamed that I had caused—and would continue to cause—my children such sadness at different times in their lives. I was seeing where I could have done things differently. I had made many bad choices andcould blame no one but myself.

What I had just seen bothered me deeply. I felt great remorse at that point. "Clearly it would have been better in some ways if I had not had to see all this," I thought, "But this was my burden to bear." I saw my life as I had lived it: hard, angry, resentful, and blind.

Then I saw a pretty young woman walking up to me— it was my sister Pamela. She had died at birth, leaving my mother completely devastated. I was a baby myself at the time Pamela had died. I saw now how hard it was for Mama to care for me because of the loss of my sister; I'd had no knowledge of this when I was alive. For the first time, I realized what my mother had gone through.

I felt a love, compassion, and understanding for Mama that was so strong. Pamela told me that it was a part of life's lessons that was needed at that time. She told me she had wanted to be the one to come to Mama, even if it was only for a short time, and that she was glad to see me again. Then as quickly as she was there she was gone.

Then I saw the hell that I had caused my mother when I was thirteen. I don't know how she survived it all. I saw where I had hardened my heart and was brutal toward her for all the pain that I had felt, blaming her for all that had ever hurt me. I felt so ashamed of myself for what I had done to her. As I stood there, reviewing my life, I could feel that I was receiving comfort from the Comforter. The Guardian's thoughts seemed to intertwine with mine—it was the most amazing experience I had ever had! All that had happened to me, and everything that I saw, I held very sacred in my heart, sealed away in my memory.

Then a brilliant light came from all corners. More light than I had ever seen was there in my sight. The brightness of the light, the brilliance of the love, and the manifestation of all my dreams were there for me to understand. All of these things were rolled into one and permeated my very existence. As the Guardian and I moved along, I saw what looked like a city of lights off in the distance. Its enormous size still boggles my mind. Such splendor I had never seen before.

All of a sudden the Guardian and I seemed to be moving across water. I looked down to see my feet only slightly touching the water. I was totally amazed at this. As the water crossed over the top of my feet, I thought to myself, "I only knew of one that could do this. He had walked on the waters to still them; He was there to take fear away from His brothers."

The Guardian answered my thought with the words, "Here, you are as one, with one, to be one. Remember this always."

I knew that I would. Then I thought, "I wonder if Jesus felt the same way as I do now."

"*Yes,*" was the reply I heard in my mind.

I felt so humbled at the thought that I could be in the same place as Him. As we moved across the water to the land in front of us, there was a path we chose to take. I saw a huge building with many stairs in front of it. We seemed to effortlessly follow them to the very top. There were six large pillars in the front of this building that reminded me of Greek architecture. They formed long columns, like hallways inside, although I never saw a wall or a roof.

As we moved inside, I stopped to touch one of the tall, beautiful pillars with my right hand. They seemed to look like large blocks of light and yet they were very solid and carved to perfection. Almost instantly after touching the pillar, there was a depth of knowledge that surged deep inside of me, a vibration that went to the very core of my soul. It was as if I were a sponge that absorbed all of the knowledge it held inside.

We moved into a room. Water flowed from the front of the room, through the middle of this room, and down blocks that looked like a staircase. The light that was in the water was as if it were generating a life force of some kind.

I said to the Guardian, "Why can't I see anyone? I know there are people here, I can feel them."

"Maybe you are looking with your eyes instead of your heart," He said to me.

I did as He asked, and I began to see. I saw what appeared to be pews lined up row after row. That's when I started recognizing the people that were sitting there. My Mom, both of my Gramma's, my Uncle, my Aunt, and even the neighbor lady that had lived across the street from Mama; I knew many that were there. They were all together there, sharing the knowledge of the Keys of Life's Existence and much more.

I asked the Guardian, "Why won't they come close to me?"

Then I heard, "Shhh. . . . Karen's not ready yet."

I thought to myself, "Yes, I'm ready!"

I knew that I had learned all of the Keys. There was love, kindness, compassion, forgiveness, selflessness, benevolence, friendship, gratitude, humility, non-condemnation, peaceful serenity, sharing respect for others, self respect, praise, openness of spirit, truth, and caring for your fellow man.

"I could have developed my gifts. If only I had at least tried to make more of an effort in my life than I had. *We are all meant to be powerful individuals.*" I thought to myself. I was amazed at the way I could see and feel and understand it all. At that point again I asked God to forgive me for all of my foolish ways. Everything I had done in my life had shown me that I had not been as loving as I needed to be. I felt His love and comfort at that moment. *As we are part of the Creator Himself, so I could re-create.* I hoped the Guardian knew that the keys had opened up everything for me to understand now.

"But why wouldn't the others talk to me?" I wondered. "Why wouldn't they come close to me?"

The light became brighter as we moved to the next place, swiftly and easily, gliding into a shade of deep purple and blue. It was as if we were gliding through another galaxy or dimension. We came to be in this beautiful meadow that was full of flowers which embraced the ground like a blanket. We were going down a path through the meadow to another place. The path was golden in color with a reddish tint to it and it sparkled like glitter had been cast over it. I reached down to pick some flowers, they were just gorgeous. To my surprise what I had just picked with my hand grew right back in the same place.

The Guardian's thoughts again came to me, and He simply said, *"Karen, there is no death."* These flowers in my hand were an expression of love and life for being a part of all that is. It was as if they were breathing with a pulsating life force.

As I looked at them they had was a softness like velvet, and appeared as if dew were on them. As I held them close to me they became one with me. I could feel their beauty inside me. I was learning to enjoy the pleasure of pure beauty.

I suddenly realized that I *could* create God's love. I felt set apart from who I had been in my life review. *The Keys to life were inside of me, where they had been all along.* I knew that spiritual growth was necessary, and the only way to achieve it was to live a physical life. I had not lived mine in a constructive manner. In many ways I had failed myself, my family and the few people in my life that meant anything to me.

It was an awakening that I will never forget. *I could have done better, I should have done better.* I realized that I had blown my chance in so many ways, so many times. Whether good or bad, I saw my life for what it really was. The lessons that I needed to learn had shown themselves clearly to me here.

We moved forward to the next crystal room, I could hear different languages. "Funny," I thought, "I can understand what I am hearing." Although I had never learned different languages, I seemed to just know them.

There in that room I saw things that made me feel very sad. I saw faraway lands that I had never seen before. They were in total devastation. I saw many scenes of desperation. I saw an island completely submerged by water and what appeared to be hundreds, if not thousands, of people missing and the island that they lived on ceased to exist. Feeling somewhat overwhelmed by all that I saw I asked the Guardian, "Why am I seeing this? What can I do?"

Again the Comforter comforted me, soothing my spirit.

We entered another room and I was shown many different things. People starving, Land that used to be rich now parched. Waterways that had changed their courses, Volcanoes emerging from waters that had never had them before, Medications being discovered but not used to cure some diseases. I saw many things that I was able to understand. The images came quickly and then they were gone almost as swiftly as they had come. Then we left the room. I only knew that my heart was heavy with so many things at that point.

"What could I do?" I thought to myself. I wanted desperately to do something, but what? How? I didn't know. I realized coming away from this place that I had learned compassion on a scale that I had never realized before.

As we moved away from this place I looked back, still feeling moved by what I had seen. I was looking ahead of us and the light was so bright it was as if I were looking directly into the sun. I knew *this was God*, I felt His presence all around me.

Then the Guardian's thoughts intermingled with mine, "Karen, if you had the chance would you change anything?"

Without hesitation, I jumped right on it. "Oh my God . . . YES! In a heartbeat!" (It wasn't God that I was talking to, but He was there. He had permeated the very existence of who I was and who I could be.) I answered, "The first thing I'd do is love my kids better, and other people as well."

"Why would you do that?" was His reply.

"Because that is the Creator's intent for us; to love as He has loved us, to be compassionate and caring, to help each other and learn. I've seen where I didn't show love to many people in my life, including my two children. I would help my children feel love, and show them how to receive it."

God had opened up my eyes, to show me that I could do this and do it well. I was ashamed that I had not cared for my children in the way that I should have. But that was my thought, not anyone else's judgment of me. My children had not gotten the best from me, and I now regretted it. I wanted to show them how to love and be loved and to accept love. "So the first thing that I would do is love both of my kids better," I said.

"Is there anything else?" the Guardian asked.

"Oh yes!" I said, "I would help people whenever I could, however I could, and for whatever reason, as long as it was for the good of mankind and for God's sake."

He never said another thing to me.

All at once everything around me went black. I heard a roaring sound in my ears again. I felt like I was on my back up in the air, like I was being pushed into an awfully small space that I didn't really fit into. I was way too big for this area. Harder and harder I felt pushed inside. I didn't want to be there; it hurt to be pushed on so hard. Then I felt a horrible pain in the front of my chest. I was being pushed back into my physical body! The pain was unbearable. The buzzing in my ears was so loud it was as if there were a thousand bees inside of my head. I was back on the cement floor in the boiler room. My chest felt like it was caving in. I could taste blood in my mouth where I had hit it or bitten it. I wasn't sure what had happened.

"Oh Lord!" I cried out.

I felt so much pain. I never felt so bad in all my life. *Where was the Guardian?* I couldn't see him anymore. Where was He?

"Oh God this hurts please make it stop," I prayed, but nothing changed. I felt so much confusion at that moment. I kept thinking to myself, "Please take me back! I don't want to do this . . . Okay! I don't want to be here! I didn't want to come back! I didn't ask to come back here . . . Or did I? Where did the Guardian go? Where was my beautiful place? Why am I here? Where is the beautiful place that I was standing in? WHAT IS GOING ON?"

I was so upset at this point.

Then it hit me . . . *Man what the heck is that smell?* It was me. That's when I noticed that I had messed on myself and wet my pants. "Oh gads, Oh my gads," I thought, "I am a nasty stinking mess!" The thoughts were still racing through my mind. "Where is the Guardian? Why am I here instead of there?" I felt so confused. I knew I had just been there, I just didn't understand how I got here. But where was I?

My chest felt like it was on fire inside, my breathing was very labored. I thought to myself, "Maybe I can just die and get this all over with." But my body wouldn't hear of it. It was fighting so hard for every breath. I had no control over my body. It was fighting to stay alive. I was so thirsty that my lips were stinging. I ran my tongue across them and felt the cracks in my skin. They were chapped real bad.

I thought, "How could He do this to me?" The tears ran down my cheeks as I started trying to move. "I remember Him loving me and I was in the most wonderful place, wasn't I? Of course I was there but where was He now?"

I began to crawl out of the boiler room and that's when I looked up at the wall to see the clock. "That can't be right," I thought to myself.When I had gone into the boiler room it couldn't have been much later than five-twenty or so, and it was now a few minutes before seven a.m. I had somehow lost roughly an hour and a half. Had I been with the Guardian that long?" Now I was even more confused. I pulled myself up on one of the washing machines in the Laundromat area and took a few steps, I was having a very hard time breathing.

Then I heard a pecking sound coming from the front of the building. I saw the seamstress' husband through the glass door—he had come to pick up the mending for the week and had seen the lights on so he went ahead and stopped in.. He was knocking on the glass, smiling as he waved at me. When our eyes met, he knew something was terribly wrong with me.

I motioned him toward the side door; I had left it unlocked. He was an older fellow, but you would have never known it that morning. He ran inside to try to help me get outside into the fresh air. As I tried to catch my breath, he asked me if I was having an asthma attack. I shook my head "no." I couldn't talk at all. It was taking every ounce of strength I had just to try to lean up against the wall outside in the drive through.

My legs were real shaky, but I couldn't sit down. I was sick at my stomach. Every time I bent over I couldn't breathe and my breathing would get worse. So I leaned up against the wall, huffing and puffing.

Again he asked, "Are you having and attack?"

I nodded my head up and down *"yes."* I had remembered that my brother's stepdaughter Lisa had left her asthma medicine in my car. She always carried her inhaler with her. I whispered to him, "Medicine," and I pointed toward the car.

That old man took off running like he had fire on his tail. He jumped a three-and-a-half-foot drop off getting down to where my car was parked out in the lot. He got inside my car and saw the medicine. It was there in plain view in the catch-all caddie in the center of the floorboard. He ran it back up to me and I inhaled it as fast as I could. I don't know how many times I inhaled that darn thing. No sooner had I taken a puff than I took another and another. I had never been on any inhalers of any kind but I thought it would make me feel better, and it did help me over the next little while to open up my throat so that I could breathe better. Little by little, I got to where I could talk in between gasps for air. Slowly what had happened was starting to make a lot more sense to me. I had messed on myself. I was also wet and I was very embarrassed by it all. All I wanted to do was to go home and clean up.

I was still breathing pretty rough, but I tried to explain what had happened to me. By this time, Susan and Dan had made it to work.

I told Dan and Susan about the mess that had been left behind for me to clean up, and about all the dirty rags that I had used. I had put them all inside the dry cleaning machine to recycle the *Perk* that I had cleaned up off the floor. Someone had used the *Devour* that weekend—there were two empty containers of it in the trash—but there was no evidence of the rags that had been soaked in the darn stuff, 'cause I had already put them into the dry cleaning machine.

Dan went and emptied the bucket that I had poured the chemical into. I didn't want anyone else to get hurt with that darn stuff—unfortunately, that meant that later there would be no evidence except Dan admitting that he poured out some chemicals that I had mixed in the bucket.

I knew there had to have been *Devour* in that bucket. It all made perfect sense to me—the rags, the empty containers of *Devour*; why didn't I pay more attention? There must have been more than one chemical inside that bucket. I had poured the powdered bleach into the bucket, but there must have been some other chemicals in there from someone else using the bucket; that's why it had made a toxic steam when I'd added water. It was the protein-eating agent, the *Devour,* that got to me. I knew it deep down inside of me. The only time that I had ever had a bad physical reaction was when that chemical was used around me, and I had not used it. I had put chemicals into the bucket, myself, but it wasn't *Devour,* just a real strong bleach.

I was in sad shape. I was embarrassed about how I looked and smelled. I just wanted to go home and clean myself up. I was so upset but I wasn't scared. I just didn't understand what all had happened to me. I wanted to go back to where I'd been with the Guardian but I wasn't for sure where that was. But how did I get back here? There were a lot of questions that were left unanswered. "Why me," I thought? I hadn't asked for this . . . or did I?

The Beginning of My New Life

I DIDN'T KNOW WHAT WAS GOING ON INSIDE OF me. When I got home, all I could think about was the Guardian. I was trying to clean myself up, and I kept having to stop and catch my breath. It took about two hours just to get clean and change my nasty clothes—it felt like forever. I kept remembering Him. I was thinking that I must be nuttier than a fruitcake, but I knew I had gone *somewhere*. I *knew He was there with me*; I just knew it, no ifs, ands or buts. I was remembering all kinds of stuff, but none of it seemed to make a whole lot of sense at the moment.

The inside of my body felt as though it had been destroyed. My gut feeling told me I was in serious trouble. I kept telling myself I'd be all right; I just needed to get my head back on my shoulders and get my act together. My breath was still very shallow. My lungs felt as though they were burning inside real bad. I didn't think I was hurt that bad . . . or maybe I chose not to want to believe what had happened to me was that serious.

I had always been as strong as a mule, but I knew I needed to see a doctor. I'm from the generation that says 'don't stop till you drop,' but I was so wiped out all I wanted to do was lay down and rest. By the time I finished cleaning myself up, I was completely worn out. I could hardly move, I hurt so bad.

I walked into the front room. I thought I would stretch out on the couch for a while, and found out the hard way that I couldn't lay down . . . at all! When I tried to lay down on the couch, it felt like I was one big blister inside, like something was crushing in my ribs when I tried to lay flat. I rolled off the couch onto the floor on my hands and knees. I was struggling for the smallest amount of breath. It felt like my lungs just weren't getting any air in them at all. It took me several minutes before I could finally breathe a little easier.

"Why . . . Oh God why . . . did I have to come back like this? Why did he leave me like this?" I thought to myself.

I made it to a chair at the dining room table and sat down, crossing my arms in front me. I rested my head on them and the tears began rolling down my cheeks and across my arms. I realized right then and there I gotta quit crying, this isn't gonna help. I couldn't' breathe through my nose and the tears were only adding insult to injury. I didn't have any health insurance and I was concerned about how this was going to affect my job and my boss. It would take me almost a year before I could even lay down in my own bed to sleep or try and rest. I stayed in a chair for the better part of five months after the accident.

I didn't know what was going on inside of me back then. I wasn't aware of the change that had taken place within me yet. The person I am now isn't the person that I was then. My brain was thinking one way and my body was feeling another.

I missed many days of work and my boss was getting nervous. The work was backing up on him and he wasn't too happy about my health. I tried going back to work, but that sure didn't last long. My lungs hurt so bad just trying to breathe the air in that place. I think at that point was when they realized—and so did I—that I was hurt a lot worse than we all had thought.

Of course there were some that thought I was just putting-on-the-dog. I really tried to go back, and to work an hour here and there, but I couldn't cut it; the exertion of just walking into that place was more than I could take. Many times I asked myself, "Why did I come back?" I told the kids at work I was afraid that I was really messed up.

Dan was a great young man to work with. He had a wife and two children. He was trying to finish college to become a Social Worker. He had worked for my boss for several years. (I knew some-how that he was asthmatic.)

"This place and the chemicals are slowly gonna kill ya' if you stay here." I told him. "*Pleeease* quit while your ahead; it ain't worth giving your life for some stinking dirty clothes."

He knew that I had been as healthy as a mule before this had happened to me. We started looking in the safety book that contained all the side effects and hazards with the particular chemicals we had been working with. The *Devour* wasn't even posted in the book yet. The other chemical (carbon tetrachloride) that I had been using was highly toxic. Only half of the side effects were in print in the Safety Manuel. Later I would find out that I should have been wearing an oxygenated face mask with one of the chemicals I had been using because of its high toxicity level. Dan quit his job at the cleaners a few days later. I didn't feel guilty at all, in fact I felt pretty darn good . . . for him. At least there would be one person that would be saved from this chemical. At least this would not happen to him.

My co-worker, Susan, suggested that I call Ask-a-Nurse and see if they could offer some kind of help for me. So I did. She asked for all of my physical symptoms and I told her: my fingers were tingling along with my elbows, and it felt like ants were crawling on my back. Headache, nausea, burning; take your pick, I had them all.

The nurse immediately said I needed medical attention. I told her I had used someone else's Provental inhaler and it had helped me to regain my breath many times since the accident. She said that it was real risky for me to use someone else's medicine and advised me to see a doctor right away. I told her I didn't have one, so she gave me a choice of three doctors with new practices. I picked one and called to make an appointment.

Several days after the accident I went into work and tried to fill out all the necessary papers. Julie was there, and I wasn't getting too good of a response from her when I started telling her what had happened to me. I knew that it was the one chemical left in the bucket that fried my lungs. She didn't say much, but she didn't have to; I knew she felt guilty since she was the one that had used the *Devour* and left it in my bucket. All my emotions came to the surface and I just started crying and asking her why in the heck she brought that stuff in here. She said she just didn't think. She quit her job a few weeks after the accident.

I finally got to go in to see a doctor, and the nurse practitioner talked to me first. She asked me questions about smoking. I told her I had been a smoker for years, but that I had also quit a few years earlier. I felt that I was in good shape until this happened. Just a few days before the accident, my daughter and I had walked and jogged to Sugarhouse Park, trying to keep in shape. I had always been in decent shape 'cause I had always been active. There wasn't much that I hadn't done or tried to do physically, from riding dirt bikes to bowling. I even drove an eighteen-wheeler that pulled a 45' x 102' flat bed (that I owned) to hauling shake-n-bake (glycerin in carefully packed 45' foot cylinders), and had put together a swing set for my Granddaughter. I prided myself in thinking that I was stronger than most women my size and not afraid to do most anything. "Tell me I can't do something and I'll show you I can," that was my attitude until this happened.

I explained to the nurse about the chemicals that I had used and those that I had been exposed to, as well as the incident with the bucket. She said she would have to check with Poison Control to see what their input was. She felt that I had severely burned my lungs.

Poison Control agreed that I had been exposed to some highly toxic stuff. I had all the symptoms of being poisoned and burned. While I was there, I had many tests that the doctor had ordered. Afterward the nurse took some blood and gave me a breathing test. Boy there sure wasn't very much air coming in or out of my lungs at all.

When she left the room, I was in a daze. I sat in the room by myself wondering why in the heck this had to happen. I never thought anything like this would have happened to me, and then I started getting flashbacks of being there with Him.

Then I heard voices coming from out in the office area. The door was slightly ajar, and I could hear clearly what was being said in the outer room. The Nurse Practitioner was explaining to the doctor that she had contacted Poison Control and they had confirmed that my symptoms were that of being poisoned, and that she had made me aware of what they had said. He began to rake her over the coals, he told her to never do that kind of thing again or she would be terminated; and then it was quiet.

Since the accident, I couldn't lie flat at all. I sat up in bed, propped up. I tried to tell the doctor that it felt like I would just stop breathing when I laid flat. He just looked at the floor as he listened to me. I tried to tell him all the details of what had happened to me. I even told him that I felt like I had been slowly poisoned at my job. I started to explain to him about what I could remember, but it all came in bits and pieces—back then my memory was like scrambled eggs. I knew it wasn't making any sense to him.

I guess he did all he thought he could do at that point. He gave me some prescriptions, patted me on the leg and said, "I'm sorry, there is nothing that we can do for you." I knew he thought that I had went crackers, I could feel him inside of me—somehow, I just knew what he was feeling.

I told him that I would get real clammy and sweaty, and about the buzzing in my head and about the high pitched sound in both of my ears. I felt like someone was charging me with battery cables most of the time. He didn't understand what I was trying to explain to him. He proceeded to tell me that I had fried my lungs from smoking! And that this accident had aggravated my condition of *chronic emphysema.*

I had no idea what he was talking about. None of this made any sense to me at all! I had not ever had to take any kind of medicine for this so-called condition that he said I had; my past medical records would testify to that. When I was driving truck the year before I had to take a two year health check and no one had mentioned anything to me about this. Suddenly I felt like I was on trial for having had an accident on the job. I could not believe my ears! This man was telling me that I was dying; that I might only have a few weeks to, live and he was sorry!

The worst part about it all was the fact that he said it wasn't caused from my work or the chemicals. I was in a complete daze. I didn't have any medical insurance and now this doctor was saying that I had aggravated a condition that I didn't even know that I had. I didn't know what I was gonna do. I couldn't work, and now there wasn't even gonna be Worker's Compensation for the accident. I couldn't walk two steps without wheezing and loosing my breath. I felt like miss huff-and-puff. My lungs ached so bad that I prayed for death but it never came. What was I going to do now? Just a few days before I was fine and very healthy; this didn't make any kind of sense at all.

The doctor wrote a letter to my boss permanently disabling me. Great, I never expected this in a million years. I couldn't file for unemployment 'cause I had a job, and if I quit I couldn't get unemployment insurance. I'm wasn't gonna get Workman's Compensation 'cause the doctor said that I had a pre-existing condition—what else was going to drop on my head?

I wasn't trying to hurt anybody, but my boss didn't see it that way at all. All he saw was a lawsuit and the loss of a worker, not someone's life. I still can't believe the way he talked to me the day I went into his office. I said to him, "You know, these are some dangerous chemicals, Tim; they need to be taken off the market as soon as possible before they kill someone else."

He glared at me from behind his desk and said, "That sounds like a personal *threat* to me."

"Man, what's the matter with you!" I said, "Do you think I wanted to be like this for a few bucks? Come on, cut me some slack Tim, these chemicals killed me—do you realize what I'm saying to you at all? I thought you knew me better that." I told him if there was any way I could stop the use of these dangerous chemicals I'd sure as heck do it!

He looked at me and said, "That sounds like a threat to me if I ever heard one."

I just couldn't believe my ears. I continued, "Look, all I need is a little help with my medical expenses. I'm not trying to get to you."

He said, "Sounds like you have a personal problem here."

I started crying, I couldn't believe how unfair everything seemed to be. I knew at that point I wasn't going to get any help from him or anyone else. I walked out of his office feeling about as low as bird's doo-doo that day.

I needed to accept the fact that I had my lungs were ruined. The doctor had told me my lungs were shot. His expectations for me were not good and he gave me a short time to live. He had given me a couple of inhalers and sent me home . . . to die.

I just couldn't understand how all of this could have happened. I needed another opinion. With no Workers Compensation checks and no unemployment insurance, there was no were to turn. My little bit of savings was going fast and all I had was a credit card. So I took out some money against the card. I know that wasn't too wise, but at that point I didn't think I had any other choice—what were they gonna do put me in jail?

I went to another doctor and he gave me the same diagnosis, although he added a little more time for me to live. In the meantime I was running out of money, living off a credit card, and my patience with life . . . was gone.

"Why couldn't I just die and get it over with?" I thought.

The system we all live in can have its drawbacks at times. I needed help, but I was running into roadblocks left and right. In the meantime, my daughter whom I was living with didn't make enough money to support me along with her own responsibilities of being a single parent. Things started getting pretty tight—not to mention the fact that my daughter thought I had fallen off the turnip truck. As time went by my memory of the other side kept taunting me. It had been several weeks since my accident.

One day I decided to try to tell my daughter Kim about my journey—or dream, as she called it later. She listened for a few minutes. The minute I started explaining the silky flesh and the Guardian she abruptly said, "Mother, we need to get in touch with your doctor, I think you need medication, I think you're hallucinating."

I shut my mouth after that, not saying another word to anyone about my thoughts or my experience. My daughter and I had not had a strong relationship, and through the years it had almost diminished. I didn't know how to tell her I was different, that I had changed. I didn't know what to say. I didn't know anyone in Salt Lake City. I hadn't really had enough time to make any friends except for the people that I worked with, and now that was gone as well.

The weeks started rolling by and I was running out of options and money. It was very hard for me to get any sleep. I rarely knew what rest was anymore. My eyes looked like two big ol' sink holes. Staring back at me in the mirror was a woman I didn't recognize at all. My mind seemed to have so much clutter and confusion inside. My thoughts were of so many different people, people that I didn't even know. I felt so bewildered most of the time. I left the light on at night 'cause I felt unsure of myself. I just didn't understand the transition or the process that was going on inside of me.

I hadn't been able to lay down flat in the bed since the accident. I told the doctor, but he said there was nothing he could do. So at night when I would go to bed, I would put my pillows all around me and leaned up against the wall to sleep; I was in a sitting position most of the time. There were times that I would wake up hearing somebody talking to me and I was answering 'em. Other times I would be sound asleep and it was as if I had been running or something in my mind. My heart would be racing so fast that I could hear my heartbeat pounding in my ears. Sweat would roll down the sides of my face like I had been crying. Other times I would feel like I was being jolted through a porthole of some kind. It was very frightening to me. I would pray to God to help me through it all. And then I would remember Him . . . then it didn't seem to be as bad as it had minutes earlier. I just wanted to tell somebody so bad about all the stuff that was in my head.

I asked God, "Please, won't ya just pull my ticket and let's get this ride over with, okay? It would be okay with me, 'cause nothing is making any sense to me." I pleaded with Him, "God, can we just do that. . . . Okay?" But it didn't happen.

Then I would think about where I had gone. Back then I wasn't sure about a lot of things. I thought that I was nuttier than a fruit cake most of the time. I remember thinking back to when I was younger and Mama would say to me, "Gal . . . it's one thing to talk to ya self, it's another if ya start answering back." Why would I remember something like that . . . now? Something had to give.

A lot of images started coming to my memory. I remembered so many different kinds of things. Pictures and places that I had never been in my life; people that I never knew bringing words to my mind that didn't make sense. Then I began to notice that whatever I had seen in my thoughts would happen not long after, like a visual déjà-vu.

Saying Goodbye

BEFORE MOVING BACK TO UTAH IN MARCH OF 1993, I had been running the forty-eight states in an eighteen-wheeler I owned. My mama had asked me to come back home 'cause she was missing me. So I took a job for a few years driving for a local company, and stopped in Utah to see my daughter every chance I got. I was really missing her a lot. I knew she needed me to be there for her, and living on the road was hard for me. When I came back from a visit with her, I knew exactly what I needed to do—I needed to move to Salt Lake City. Mama called me crazy and said that I would be better off to stay where I was at 'cause I was doing so well for myself there.

I told her, "Mama, you have stood by me all your life, what's the difference in me doing that very same thing for my own daughter?" She just didn't want me to leave her. Now I understand why, but back then it was a different story all together.

My younger brother Tony and oldest sister Almeta decided that they wanted to move to Utah as well. The thoughts were flying high at all the changes that we where wanting to make with one another. Mama was really upset with me for talking them into moving to Salt Lake City with me. I asked Mama if she would consider moving too. She just fired off at me sayin, "H---, no," and that was that, she didn't want to talk about it at all.

Over the next little while, my sister Almeta sold her house and we moved in with each other, planning on moving before winter set in. I continued to work for the trucking company and started saving money for the move. I would go over to Mama's a lot to visit and she would say, "I sure wish you guys would stay, you know me and your Daddy ain't getting any younger. I think you are making a big mistake you know." Daddy told her to mind her own business, and she would light into him telling him that he just didn't understand a mother's love. He just shook his head back and forth and shuffled out to the backyard to watch the birds.

I would just tell her how much I loved her for sticking by me for all these years, and that I was just trying to do the same thing for my daughter. As I headed out the door one evening, I said. "You know, Mama, if it wasn't for you standing beside me all these years, I don't know what I would have done." I hugged her, and then the subject was dropped and never brought up again.

A few days later, Mama started going through her things. She gave all of us something of hers. I knew I had broken Mama's heart, but that was not my intention at all. I know deep down inside she knew how much I would always love her.

The day we left sure was hard on all of us. Mama started crying, and I was trying so hard to be strong and not break down. I didn't want to cry. I knew it would only make things worse. The lump in my throat made it difficult to swallow and I was fighting the tears back so hard. I had told Mama that I would be back in a few weeks to straighten out a few loose ends and for her to not worry. She hugged Almeta and my niece Opal then she headed for me. She was crying so bad as she put her arms around my neck. I could feel her quiver inside as I put my arms around her. She said, "I ain't ever gonna see you again."

It was like I had a sick feeling in my stomach. "Ah Mama," I reassured her, "I'll be back in just a few short weeks, honest. I promise I'll take care of everything that I can when I get back."

She wouldn't let go of me, she just hung on real tight. "I love you," she said, "You remember that okay, I love you?"

"I love you too and I'll see you soon Mama okay?" I said as I hugged her hard. She was shaking so bad I was afraid she was gonna fall down.

Daddy would not come outside at all. He never liked good-byes, so he waved from the door. As he walked away, I could hear him blowing his nose; we used to tease him about sounding like a fog horn.

As I got up in the truck I looked back at Mama and yelled out, "I'll see you in a few weeks . . . I promise." She was very red faced and I didn't know what else to do. I don't think there was anything else that I could have said or done at that point.

Looking back on the day that we left has been my saddest memory of all. Back then none of us were doing a very good job of cutting the apron strings. I was feeling pretty guilty. Here I had talked my oldest sister, Almeta, and my only brother, Tony, into moving to Salt Lake City. My kid sister was the only one to stay behind with Mama. My brother had already left for Utah a few weeks before, so he didn't see how Mama reacted that day, but my sister and I did. It's funny how we think we know what will make us happy until we lose everything that ever meant anything to us.

✳

I'll never forget the words Mama said to me, "I'm never going to see you again." As I look back now I realize she must have known something that we didn't; call it pre-monition or intuition, I don't know, but Mama knew. When Mama passed away a few weeks later we were all in shock!

I've heard it said that you should try to prepare and give yourself time to adjust when someone dies. There is never enough time for that, each person is different—although I have found that time is more of a great healer than we realize. We had talked to Mama on her birthday the 29th of April and she was complaining of her stomach bothering her. She thought it was the flu. Then my little sister Lynette called us to let us know Mama was in the hospital. She had started hemorrhaging internally. She was very weak and frightened.

We were all together, trying to hurry and get to her. Mama knew that we were all on our way. My little sister told Mama to hang on that all of us would be there soon. We tried to catch a flight, but due to Almeta's physical size we couldn't get a seat on the airplane big enough for her, so I rented a car and we all took off for California. Almeta was so embarrassed that we had to rent a car to take her with us. She wanted my brother and I to fly out ahead, but we couldn't leave her behind. She had always been big, but now she was about five-hundred pounds, maybe more. We chose to drive so we could all go together. I told everyone to hang on 'cause I wasn't gonna waste any time on the road. The trip was about a twelve-to-fourteen hour shot from Salt Lake City, and I wasn't gonna let much grass grow under my feet getting there.

We all left Salt Lake at around five o'clock that afternoon. At one point Almeta said, "Sis if you want to . . ."

I just looked at her and said, "Don't even go there, we are all going together and that's that."

It was getting late and everyone in the car was asleep. I was still driving hard. I looked down at the clock, it was almost 1:00 a.m. It was pitch black out there in the Nevada desert. Up ahead I saw what appeared to be someone standing in the middle of the dad-gum road. I looked back at the clock it was five minutes after one. I couldn't believe my eyes. I rubbed them because I thought that I was seeing things. There, in the middle of the I-80 Highway about twenty or so miles out of Sparks, Nevada, was *Mama*! She was standing there in the middle of the road waving at me! It looked as though she was wearing a pretty aqua nightgown and a smile as big as life itself. My foot slipped off the accelerator and the car started slowing down. I just watched her, she looked so beautiful and peaceful, and then she was gone. Everyone started waking up in the car when they felt it slowing down.

I knew at that moment our mother had crossed over. I pulled off to side of the road and got out of the car; I needed to get some fresh air, fast. I leaned up on the side of the car looking out into the night where Mama had been standing there in the roadway. My brother Tony had gotten out of the car as well and asked me if I was ready for him to take over driving I kept looking out into the night, tears rolling down my cheeks. I simply said to him, "There ain't no reason to rush anymore." He just stared at me in disbelief.

Almeta asked what was wrong the minute I got back into the car. I told her I had seen Mama standing out in the middle of the road, and I thought Mama had passed away. Almeta just looked at me and started to cry. She turned her head toward the window and never said another word.

For the next four and a half-hours none of us said anything. We arrived at my kid sister's house around 5:30 that morning. When she came outside crying, we knew our worst thoughts were true. Later that morning, Almeta, my niece, Opal, Tony, and myself drove into Stockton to Mama's house. This time it was different. My brother was taking it very hard, so he went over to a buddy's house around the corner from Mama's. He just couldn't go inside Mama's house without her there. Daddy had stayed at my kid sister's 'cause he wasn't doing very good himself. It had been a horrible night for my sister and Daddy. When we arrived at Mamas' house and went inside, I could smell Mama's perfume throughout the house. "Holy mackerel," I said, "That perfume sure is strong, huh Almeta!" As I walked through the front room, I turned around to see Almeta looking at me kind of funny.

She asked me, "What ya smelling, Sis?"

"What do you mean, what am I smelling?" I said, "It's Mama's perfume, of course. Can't you smell it?"

"Just faintly," she said as she sat down in a daze at the dining room table.

I started looking for where the aroma was coming from and Opal, my niece, was right behind me. For everyone else, the smell didn't seem to be that strong. For me it was so strong it was like a bottle of perfume had been broken.

None of the others would go into Mama's bedroom. For years it had been off limits to all of us kids. We had been talking earlier about what to dress Mama in, so I said I'd check out her closet to see if she had anything that would work. When I opened the door to go into the room, *there was Mama!* Everything around me suddenly seemed to whirl. *Mama was sitting at the foot of her bed!* I was stunned to see her there!

"Are you all right, Aunt Karen?" my niece asked as she touched my arm.

I said, "Do you see anyone in there, Opal?"

"No," she replied, "But you know, I can smell Grandma's perfume now real good, and it sure feels chilly in here, huh?"

Mama just seemed to move so easily. I was so overwhelmed to see her I was weak in my knees. I had to take a step backward to lean up against the wall. I sucked in enough air for eight people at that point. I felt like I was going to fall down right there on the spot.

Opal asked, "Are you okay?"

I looked at her and said, "Yeah, I think so, but you're going to think I'm nuttier than a flipping fruit cake!"

"Why is that?" she asked.

"Opal, do you see anything in Mama's room?" I asked.

She looked in the room, then back at me, and said, "No . . ."

"Well I do," I said, "Mama's in there!" Then Mama started telling me where she had different things hidden. I could feel her somehow. I told Opal.

Opal looked at me kind of funny and said, "Ookkaay come on, let's go into the other room. You need to rest now, and that's all there is to it. We can do this later, okay?"

When we went in the front room, Almeta asked me if I was all right. I started telling her what had just happened. Almeta asked me what Mama had said. I told her Mama had said it was about time we got there. She had waited as long as she could, but she had to go—but there were some things that she had to tell us kids.

A funny look came across Almeta's face, and then she looked away from me with tears filling her eyes. She said she thought she had seen something in the kitchen but she wasn't for sure what 'it' was. Something . . . had caught her eye, but nothing was there.

A little bit later, I went back to Mama's bedroom again and Opal went with me. She had grabbed a pen and a tablet so she could write down everything that I would say to her. When I opened up the door . . . there was Mama! Whenever Mama wanted to get our attention, she would always call us by our first two names. She sure didn't have to do that now—she had my undivided attention!

Mama pointed to the table at the side of her bed. Opal had followed me into the bedroom so she could listen and see what ever was going to happen. I could hear what Mama was saying; her voice was ringing in my head like a steady hum. This was all very strange for Opal and I that morning. I told Opal that Mama was pointing to her nightstand; she was coaxing me to look under the doilies. I told Opal, "Mama is trying to tell me something about this table but I can't quite understand her." I looked on the top of the table, nothing was there, and then I lifted the little doilies up and there was a hundred-dollar bill! Mama showed me where she had stashed more money. She also revealed to me that other things had been taken by someone that was not a family member.

I was sure glad that Opal was in there with me. I wasn't scared—but I thought that Opal felt I was loosing it. Whatever Mama would say to me, I shared with Opal. Then Mama would show me or tell me where an item was. Sure enough, we'd find what she had said would be there! Opal was writing it all down on the pad.

This was unreal. Never in my wildest dreams would I ever have thought that I could communicate this way with Mama! For the life of me, I couldn't understand how I was able to do this, Mama was so clear to me. Opal said she didn't understand what was really going on at all. She said that all she felt was a tingling sensation and that it was a little cool in the room.

Much later Almeta, Opal, and I talked about how Mama's bedroom windows, that faced the West and always got the sun . . . how could it be so cool in the room? Mama never kept a tidy room and as she got older she turned into a pack rat. Clothes and all kind of things were piled in that little bedroom. Mama always complained that she didn't have any money to fix things around the house. She had always been on the poor side, but she showed us where lots of money was hidden.

Over the next few days, it seemed so hard for me to try to act normal. When Almeta moved to Salt Lake City with me, Mama felt she had to change the Executor of her Will from the oldest (Almeta) to my little sister (Lynette) who still lived close by. Lynette was overwhelmed by the task of getting Mama's affairs in order, so I felt like I needed to help her out. She had been here all alone in the process of Mama's death, and we all knew it had to be especially rough on her and Daddy.

We were told later that Mama really had a hard time before she died. After close to twenty hours of agony, the doctor went in for exploratory surgery, but there was nothing they could do to reverse what had happened to her. So Mama had a very painful and drawn out process to leave this world. They loaded her up on Morphine, but that really didn't help until she finally lapsed into a deep sleep from all the medicine she had been given.

Mama must have had a premonition, because thirty days prior she had bought her own funeral package. The only thing left was to pick out the clothes that she needed to wear. Now here I sat in the mortuary with my sister, trying to take care of this task. So far the only tears that I had shed were on I-80 in Nevada. I was numb to say the least. I stopped trying to explain to the others what was going on with me—they had their own grief to deal with. I know that everyone thought I had lost my mind. I didn't want them to experience any more suffering than they were already, so I figured I would keep my mouth shut.

The day of the funeral was weird. Mama was at home, yet her body was being laid to rest in a little town called Farmington, California, way out in the country. That's where her parents and other family members were laid to rest. We were all going through the motions of life, but not feeling anything but sorrow and grief. Almeta couldn't walk out to the graveside because of her unstable legs, so she sat in the car looking out across the graveyard where all of us were standing. My kid sister stood at the foot of her grave while I was by her side with my daddy.

Little by little people started to leave. I stood there looking at the flowers that us kids had given to Mama. Now it all seemed so sad to see how hard her life had been lived and the struggles that she had gone through. As I stood there, I could feel Mama telling me it would be all right and that I needed to try to keep the family together as much as possible. It was gonna be hard over the next while and I needed to do all I could to keep everyone intact, in touch, and to stay close.

I noticed dad was unsteady on his feet. I asked, "Daddy are you okay?" He just nodded his head like a little puppet up and down, staring at the casket covered in flowers. Then he stumbled toward a chair and sat down by his sister.

I could hear Mama in my head telling me that she was so surprised to see so many there. "So many people came to say goodbye, how about that!" she said. "Oh Lord," I asked, "Please help me to understand all of this, please." My head was whirling. I didn't understand what was happening. I remember turning around and walking away, when suddenly I was on the ground, face first in the grass. I felt some big fella pick me up. As I looked up I saw it was a good friend of my brothers.

As we were driving home, I was extremely ill at my stomach, I hadn't eaten in a few days. Now all of these people were there in Mama's house with food and flowers. I was just numb to what was happening, I couldn't understand it at all. People took forever to leave that day.

I asked Daddy if he wanted to lie down and he said, "Yes." Later my kid sister told us how Daddy had kept trying to wake Mama up at the hospital after she had died, and how weeks earlier Daddy had scared Mama pretty bad. He had left the burners on the top of the stove on and Mama was afraid that he was gonna burn down the house. He had burned a pot so bad that the house had a horrible smell in it for days afterward.

Mama thought that Daddy would pass away long before she would, and she lived with that fear for years. Now here we were, trying to take care of a task that depleted all of us. We all had just moved to Salt Lake City, so money was scarce. As the days went by, we thought it would be better if Daddy stayed at a retirement center close to where our younger sister lived.

The next task was to try and go through Mama's stuff. My brother and I were the ones to stay behind and take care of that detail. No one should have to go through that ordeal. We were there for thirty days, cleaning and going through it all. We drove away with thirty-five years of Mama's memories packed into a twenty-seven foot truck. As my brother and I prepared to leave, I jumped up in the truck. For a moment I had to look back. We had so many memories there. Each of us kids shared all of Mama's treasures, everyone taking something with us that belonged to her. When I drove away from the house, I looked back for the last time. I couldn't explain how, but I could see Mama and hear her talk to me. As I pulled away, she just stood there waving goodbye to me as she had so many times before.

We laid Mama to rest in May, 1993. Mama was our matriarch, our strength and our understanding. Life would never be the same for any of us kids after that. We all had adjustments to make in our personal lives after such a loss as this. We each went through the motions of existence, not knowing what was gonna happen next.

Another Family Loss

M Y FAMILY ALREADY THOUGHT I HAD LOST all concept of reality after Mama passed away. I was searching for my faith and for God. I had joined the Church of Jesus Christ of Latter Day Saints a few months after Mama's death in 1993. My sister, Almeta, had sat in on all of my home visits with the missionaries and the visiting home teachers.

For the first time in Almeta's life, she seemed to be believing that there was a God after all. Before that she had not known what to believe. She didn't know if God even existed or if he was just a figment of her imagination. The missionaries tried to talk Almeta into baptized, but she said no—she remembered getting stuck in the above-ground swimming pool in her back yard years earlier. She was extremely overweight and she couldn't pull her body weight out of the pool. Later, she said it took her husband hours to get her out. She said she felt like a beached whale and never went swimming again. So that's why she didn't want to be baptized, she didn't want to drown.

Almeta loved kids. She and her husband were only able to have one child, which was Opal. But Almeta fostered thirty-eight children before coming to Utah. She spent many hours reading the scriptures and talking with me. Those are very fond and loving memories of mine. I never thought Almeta and I could ever get any closer but we did. I know in my heart that it was real hard for Almeta to accept God as being real, but she did.

Almeta called one day and said, "You know Sis, I'm not doing so well. I don't think I'm going to make it."

I said, 'I don't even want to hear that kind of talk. All you have to do is lose a little bit of weight; you need to try to move around a little bit."

She said, "Sis, I just don't think I can." Over the next two days I didn't talk to Almeta, and the next thing I heard was that my niece had called an ambulance and Almeta was in the hospital.

Almeta called me at home. Again she said, 'Sis, I am not going to make it."

I still didn't want to hear it and I said, "Honey, you're going to be okay, you're going to be okay. I promise. I'll call you later," I told her. I never got to make that call.

On November 21st, 1994, I was in my bedroom when the phone rang. The voice said, "Ms. Baldwin, Ms. Karen Baldwin?"

"Yes," I answered, "Can I help you?"

The voice on the other end paused, "This is the doctor from the hospital. I regret to inform you that your sister, Almeta, passed away at 9:15 this evening."

'No! . . . No!" I said as I started crying and holding my head. I slid to the floor to sit down as I was crying, still hanging on to the phone.

My daughter came running into the kitchen and saw me there. "What's wrong?" she yelled out. "What's wrong Mom?" She took the phone from my hand and finished the conversation with the doctor. The hospital had been trying to locate Opal since Almeta passed. Kim told the doctor not to call my niece, but that we would like to tell her ourselves.

I sat on the floor crying, holding my head. Almeta was gone; I didn't even get to say goodbye to her, and she was all alone when she left.

Kim and I drove out to Opal's house. It was pretty late, but the lights were on when we pulled up into the driveway. Opal had turned the phone off because a prankster had been bothering her. When we got to her house, she was so surprised to see there. "Hey you guys what's up?" she said. I just looked at her with tears in my eyes. She knew as soon as she looked at me. "No, no, no!" she said. "I just left the hospital not that long ago." She grabbed onto me, crying. "I just talked to her a little while ago, she was just fine . . . How" she said?

I put my arms around her trying to console her. "Opal honey I'm so sorry, she's gone," I said gently. "The nurses had given her a sponge bath and left her in her room; when they did their rounds thirty minutes later, she was gone. Her hand was two inches away from the nurse's call button but it appeared she chose not to push it for help, I know it was her choice to leave."

The next few hours were numbing as we all went to the hospital to see Almeta. When we got there, Opal wanted to be alone with her mother. A few minutes later

I went into the room to see my Sis. There was a beautiful, soft light all around her. I bent over and kissed her on her cheek and told her how much I loved her. After several hours we all went back to our homes. It was pretty rough on all of us. Her death was so completely unexpected.

The following morning, my daughter thought it would be best that she go to work. She was so upset, but she needed to stay busy. I agreed, so I drove her to work. We were talking about Sis and how hard it was going to be on Opal. She was so young to have such a heavy load drop on her.

When I got back home, I still had Almeta on my mind. As I unlocked the door to my house, I kept thinking of the Guardian . . . and then Almeta. I walked inside the house and this anger came out of me from somewhere deep inside. I slapped my hand up against the kitchen wall. 'Doggone it Almeta, why did you give up? Why did you leave me here all alone!" I yelled out.

Then just as clear as a bell I heard her say, *"I didn't' Sis, I just got tired of being in that body."*

At that point, I literally wet my pants as I was holding onto the counter top in the kitchen. I could hear her voice just as clear as if she were standing beside me. My legs could barely keep me standing so I headed for a chair at the table. I sat down, and Almeta and I began to talk within my mind; I could hear her.

She told me she was with the Guardian and that she had a drink of the water that I had seen, (during my near death experience).

"You mean . . . the creek?" I asked.

"*Yes,*" she said "*Sis why didn't you tell me about the Guardian?*" But before I could answer her, she said, "*I understand why you didn't tell me Sis, it's okay.*"

We talked for a long time. She told me Mama was fine and that she had seen her and talked to her. Then she asked me to take care of the kids. I promised that I would. Later I wondered why she had said 'the kids,' because all she had was Opal. She also told me that her mobile home had bad wiring and that there was gonna be a fire and to be careful. I told her I would.

"*When are you gonna work?*" she said.

I didn't understand her; I couldn't work!

"*You can,*" she said. I asked her what she meant. She just said, "*You know, the gathering is at hand, and soon it will be complete.*"

She mentioned that there would be a lot of changes in the family soon, and to be strong. That a lot of people were coming into my life and it would be very fulfilling; that I would help many. I didn't understand what she meant at all. What could I do? I was barley keeping my head above the water; I didn't have a pot to whiz in or a window to through it out of!

Then she asked me if I wanted a drink . . . and laughed. I knew what she meant. When I was there I had been so thirsty but I never got a drink of water. "*Remember the creek . . . ?*" she said, "*Remember the water . . . ? Remember . . .*"

Then all of a sudden the realization hit me, I was talking to my *deceased sister*! I cried out, "Oh my God help me, please."

I immediately heard, "*I'm trying to.*"

"Please help me, oh God please," I cried. "I'm not really hearing all of this."

Again I heard, "*Yes you are.*"

"No I'm not," I said. I felt like I was going crazy. Then as quickly as Almeta had come to me, she was gone. The two worlds of spirituality and logic had started my life's direction, beginning with Mama and ending with Almeta.

I didn't know it then but my life had already started changing. My logical mind was saying I couldn't be having a conversation with my deceased sister—I had just kissed her goodbye the night before—but my heart knew differently. So the war between logic and insanity in my mind had begun.

I didn't tell anyone about the talk Almeta and I had had that day. It was hard enough to see my niece going through her grieving process. She was only 21 years old and having to deal with her mother's death and she sure didn't need me telling her this kind of stuff. So I stood by her as I had promised Almeta that I would.

Almeta passed away just nine weeks after my accident in September. Our family was getting smaller and smaller. My kid sister and Daddy flew out from California and Almeta was cremated, her ashes went home with Opal. Thanksgiving was hard 'cause we were missing two big pieces of our family. Christmas wasn't much easier, and it was the last time we would all be together. My kid sister and Daddy stayed a few days after Christmas. The day that Sis and Dad were leaving, there was a misunderstanding about when they were gonna go. My daughter kept trying to call over at my brother's house so we could see them before they left.

She wanted to take some pictures of Daddy before he took off for California, but she never got a chance.

Suddenly Kim remembered the time of their flight and the race was on. My Dad and kid sister had already boarded the plane. When we got there they allowed us to go into the plane. We walked on board, my eyes found Daddy quickly. He just looked so surprised to see Kim and I there. My kid sister looked so shocked to see us walk on board that plane 'cause it was ready to taxi out when we were allowed to go on board.

I bent over and kissed Daddy goodbye, he looked back at me with tears in his eyes. I told him, "I love you," and the tears went rolling down his cheeks.

"Me too," he said as he smiled at me.

Kim and I left the plane and they flew back to California. We were all trying to deal with our loss and the next few weeks were even more difficult.

On January 3, 1995, Daddy died in his sleep, just five weeks after Almeta. My brother called me after talking to my kid sister to tell me that Daddy had passed away. We were all devastated. I couldn't afford to fly out to California for the services. I still had no money; I was existing completely on my credit card, so I didn't even get to see Daddy or say a last goodbye.

It was unbelievable how we had lost three family members so fast and so close to one another, it was a shock for us all. In less than seventeen months we had lost our mother, our sister, and our father. My family had lost me as well since my accident—they didn't know what had happened to me, they just knew I was different, I wasn't the sister they had had all those years before.

We all had so many changes to get used to it was unreal. I know for the longest time that my family thought that I was needing medical help of some kind but they couldn't help me; their hands were full of their own emotions and I just didn't ask for anything. My health was extremely fragile now. I couldn't carry anything over three or four pounds and everything seemed like such a struggle for me. The stairs in my place were too hard for me to go up and down. It would take me forever just to get up the twenty-two stairs to go to the bathroom. I found out when I went to the grocery store that I couldn't push the cart if it got too full. For close to a year after the accident it was like that.

Gradually I seemed to get a little stronger. I would ask the clerks at the store if they would put just a few things in the bag, 'cause it made it easier for me to lift them. I felt like the plastic bag burglar most of the time! The clerks would look at me funny. I appeared healthy; I didn't have an oxygen tank yet, so they couldn't see anything physically wrong with me, I'm sure they all assumed that nothing was wrong with me.

I would try to take care of myself during the day. It would take me about an hour and a half just to clean myself. Sometimes I would sit in the tub and just let the water surround me. It would take all the strength that I had on some days just to do that. I would start to have breathing attacks that seemed to last forever. It was a good thing that I was in the tub—I would always wet on myself when the attacks came, I would just lose control. I never have had weak kidneys, but the pressure that my body was feeling at times would be very great. I wasn't getting enough oxygen. I felt like I was always breathing through a straw; there is no other way to describe it. I felt like my lungs were on fire most of the time, and after the attacks were over I felt so incredibly weak that my body would tremble uncontrollably.

I just wanted to die and get it over with. I couldn't figure out why I had to be like this. I wouldn't wish this kind of life on my worst enemy. Sometimes I just didn't want to move, I knew that I was gonna have another attack. I prayed to God asking him to please help me.

I couldn't get over my transformation, I was a completely different woman in my thoughts, I could see that for myself. The reflection in the mirror resembled me, but the woman inside was someone new and different. I had always been so healthy and strong, I couldn't believe this had happened to me. I thought for the longest time that I would wake up to find myself back home and that it was all just a bad dream, but that never happened. I had to face the facts: I was slowly dying and there was nothing that could be done for me short of a miracle.

I had been given a short time to live by the doctor, so I said to myself, "Self, we have already died once, but this dragging around just ain't getting it." I had to walk so slow. I hung onto everything that was around me 'cause I was unsure of my strength. The doctor had not prescribed oxygen for me yet, although I knew I needed it, I couldn't afford it; my credit card was paying for what medicine I was taking. The doctor was aware that I had no insurance, so I got what I got—nothing more, nothing less. It would be another nine months before I could afford to see another doctor. I was just waiting to die but that just wouldn't happen.

It was hard for me to eat a lot of the foods that I had eaten for years. I didn't like the taste of the foods that I used to *love*. I know that sounds funny, but that was the way it was. I had never been a big vegetable person; I liked fried potatoes and beans with a chunk of onion. Now I wanted different foods that I had never tasted. It was as if everything that I had liked was different now. My whole diet changed, nothing in my life was the way it had been—or at least what I was used to.

I noticed that when I was around people my mind would start racing. I felt anxious or in a hurry or something when anyone would come close to me. When we would make eye contact, the strangest things would start to happen. My heart would pound like it was coming out of my chest and I would feel so many mixed emotions. I felt so compelled to hug people and tell them everything was gonna be all right. I guess that wouldn't have been so bad if I had known these folks, but most of the time they were total strangers. I used to feel intimidated by most people, although they never knew it.

Now I could feel people deep inside of me. I seemed to know what they were uncomfortable with. It was as if their emotions were (and are) intermingled with my own and I can't break the bond—it reminds me of when I was with the Guardian how we felt with each other. I wanted so much to touch people. At times I've been afraid that they would misunderstand me, not knowing what my purpose and thoughts were. I just wanted to hug 'em and love 'em. I knew, somehow, that if I could hold them close to me for a little bit they would feel better physically or emotionally. Somehow it feels like their burdens have become my own. I knew I would be okay and their pain would go away. *I knew that* , don't ask me how I just knew.

I feel like they are small children that need a helping hand. The compassion that I feel for others is so great most of the time I just cry; I can't help it. I tell people that it isn't me . . . I know that *it is Him and that He left me with the Keys.* I just ask God to please remove their burdens. I have told people if I could have taken stock in Kleenex I'd probably be a rich person by now.

I have found one of the hardest things for me to endure is perfume. I have walked by people that smell like they've taken a bath in the darn stuff and it floors me. It tears me up; perfume has caused me to have more breathing attacks than anything else. I now have allergies out the wazoo from inside to outside—stuff that I never had before.

My eyes went bad not long after the accident as well, I now wear progressive glasses. But the neatest thing I noticed was that not too long after the accident (before I could afford glasses), whenever I would touch things I would seem to know what it said without looking at it at all. I could simply touch things with my right hand and I would know what the words said. One time I asked my daughter to read something to me. Then, as she was reading, I would mimic her and follow along with her words. I realized that I knew what it said after all. It was all so bizarre.

Kim snapped at me and say, "Well if you can read the darn thing, why did you ask me to read it to you, Mother?" Again I didn't know how to explain it. I still don't to this day—however I do use my glasses now to read.

I couldn't physically pick up my little grand baby, McKenna, anymore and boy that bothered me a lot. She couldn't understand why her "Geema," as she called me, couldn't do the things I had done before with her. I had a real hard time trying to play with her as well. I couldn't push her in a swing; two pushes would do me in and Miss huff-and-puff would strike. It was everything I could do just to walk out into the yard.

I felt so lazy just sitting all the time. I did try to write my thoughts down in a journal that I had started, only to realize that I couldn't keep up with all my thoughts. They seemed to pour out of me at such a high rate of speed.

My dog, Rusty, was even closer to me now than ever before. She gave me a lot of comfort when everyone else was griping at me. I was so glad that little dog was there with me. There were a few times that she got spooked, though. I remember one night I was breathing pretty rough and she wanted to be almost on top of my face. I'd push her away and she would come right back. I pushed her away again, then, all of a sudden, I saw Mama was standing at the foot of my bed. Rusty started wagging her tail and yelping. I really think that dog could see Mama standing there. When Mama was gone Rusty jumped off the bed and started running back and forth like she was looking for her. She was sniffing the floor and just going nuts with excitement. There had been so much grief to deal with that this was hard for me to try to explain, much less live with.

My daughter was having a great deal of difficulty dealing with everything as well. At the time she felt it would be easier if she and my granddaughter moved out of my house and got their own place. I understood why. All of us had dealt with the deaths of our family members differently. So we went our own way in March of 1995.

I had met a young girl named Mary who was very sympathetic to my situation, and she and her husband offered me a place to stay with their family; I gladly accepted. Mary, her husband and her brother-in-law moved all of my things to their house. I never let on to her what was going on inside of my mind.

The kids I moved in with were the greatest, they helped me so much. Mary and her husband were in their early twenties and had four children. Below their house, in the basement apartment, lived her sister and husband along with their two children, so there were a lot of people living in that house. My room was not attached to their house; it sat behind the garage. There was no heat in the room, just electricity, but I thought it would be all right for a little while, 'cause it was springtime.

Over the next several weeks, Mary took me to many places so that I could try to get some kind of medical help. By this time, I was looking for some new and different advice if I could find it. I had seen two previous doctors, each had given me a bleak future.

Mary offered to take me to her doctor. He was a pulmonary specialist, and she praised him so much for helping her child who had asthma. I agreed to go, I needed to see someone else. So she made an appointment for me. When I went to Dr. K, he was very pleasant to me. I told him my story, and he agreed that it sounded like the chemicals had slowly been poisoning my lungs. Mary asked him if there was any kind of a test that they could take to prove that the chemicals had indeed burned my lungs. He mentioned that there was a C.T. scan that I could have, and so he ordered one for me.

I went to a local hospital to have the test taken. It took a while to get me all plugged into this contraption. The technician asked me a lot of medical questions. I told him what had happened with the bucket and the chemicals and the exposure to Carbon Tetrachloride. I told him that before the accident, when I was still working at the cleaners, there had been three different occasions that one chemical had run me out of the building, gasping for air. I told the technician how my back used to feel like ants were crawling on it.

He shook his head and said, "That's a shame, a real shame." After the test was over, the technician came back in to see me and confirmed right then and there that he had indeed found traces of foreign matter inside my lungs—a residue indicating that I had indeed had chemicals inside of them. (This was nine months after my accident.) He patted me on the shoulder and said they would send the results to my doctor.

"What a relief," I thought. It felt good to hear that someone finally believed me. "Thank God," I said, "Someone is finally listening to me."

Mary was aware of how much I appreciated her kindness. I don't know what I could have done without her help. I will never forget them, ever.

The physician I had started seeing told me about a pulmonary rehabilitation center that he thought could help me, and gave me a prescription to go. It's one of the best here in Salt Lake City. When I arrived there, I met a lady named Connie, she was super! I was in a class with other people that had hypertension, emphysema, and asthma. We—the group of us—are all called C.O.P.D for Chronic Obstructive Pulmonary Disease. Well when I first got there, I was still huffing and puffing, walking a few feet, and then stopping to catch my breath. Connie hooked me up to a machine that would tell her what I could physically tolerate. She gave me oxygen to wear and *hot dog!* I felt like a million bucks! She put me on a treadmill and I walked as fast as I could for several minutes.

I laughed at her and said, "It's a good thing I'm in a hospital, I don't think I'm gonna get very far, I'll tell ya." She knew better. After a few minutes I was ready to call it quits.

She encouraged me to keep going and said, "Just a few more steps Karen, I know you can do it. Just a few more steps." She gave me a little more oxygen. Faster and faster she turned that doggoned treadmill up until I thought I was going to fall flat on my face. Then after what seemed to be forever, she started slowing it down. "Just a couple more steps, a few more seconds and then you'll have it," she said.

As far as I was concerned, I had had it already. But in the end she got more out of me than I ever would have thought she could. She gave me hope. I didn't think I could do it. I knew I was going to have to push myself to make it work; she told me that she knew I had it in me and she worked with me diligently. Connie said that It was apparent that I must have been in good physical shape before the accident. She also said that was good because muscle had memory and that it would bounce back. My lungs were toast, but she had faith in me physically to be able to bring back what I could and learn how to live with the difference.

Over the next few weeks she worked with me in her class. She helped me to see what I could do for myself. Time after time she would build us all up in her way to fill our own physical needs. This lady is one heck of a gal in my book. She succeeded in showing me how to take care of myself. I had finally reached a point of not waiting and wanting to die and I started learning how to live again.

Two Messages From Heaven

Nick and I had been together a few months at this time. It was February and it was as cold as a well-diggers belly button to me. He had gone to work early one morning at about 3:00 a.m. I got up about 4:30 a.m. because I was feeling a little tight in my chest. I thought it was probably the weather changing out. I thought I'd just go ahead and get up and take my shower. I was moving as slow as a snail. I had my pajamas half off and turned around and there in the doorway was Mama!

She said. "Karen, you need to start breathing better." She was standing there looking at me and talking to me! She seemed to be annoyed. She tapped the end of her nose and said, "You had better start listening, young lady." As I looked at her she was breathing in through her nose and blowing out through her mouth like she was wanting me to do the same thing. Then she said, *"Now, Karen!"*

I don't remember getting from the bathroom to the front room. The next thing I knew, I was sitting in my chair in the front room and Mama was handing me the phone. I just looked at it there in my hand.

"Honey talk to the lady now, okay?" she said.

I watched her as she headed for the front door. She turned to look back at me while unlocking the door. It flew open fast as the emergency guys came rushing inside. I was still sitting in the chair, and they whisked me onto the floor so fast. They were putting these sticky things on my chest and blowing in my mouth. I seemed to be standing beside Mama, just looking on while the emergency crew was working on me.

"If they would just leave me alone, I would be all right," I said.

Mama just tapped her nose again and said, "You really need to do this better Karen."

I watched as the paramedics put me on a stretcher and took me to the ambulance that was in the parking lot. Of all the crazy things, what was on my mind at the time was the mess they had left on the floor in my front room! They had left plastic bags and wrappers lying all over the place. Off we went to the hospital. They had me hooked up to every monitor in the ambulance. Then I heard one of the paramedics saying, "We got a pulse and it's strong." I had slipped back into my body as easily as taking in a breath.

"Stay still Karen; you'll be all right," he said.

Then it was like I was popping in and out of my body, right out of the top of my head.

The next thing I knew, I was in the emergency room and after a little while everything started to settle down around me. The doctors and nurses were just keeping a close eye on my until they got the x-rays back, then they would know more. The doctors had ordered x-rays but the ones they had taken were no good. The technician mentioned that the film must have been bad, 'cause the x-ray didn't turn out well. I asked him what the problem seemed to be.

"There is a lot of white on the film that shouldn't be there, it must have been bad film," he said. There was a white splash mark around my heart area.

I started getting shook up. I was trying to make sense of what was happening to me, but there was no logic in it. I started crying almost uncontrollably and I didn't even know why. I had been in the emergency room for several hours by now and no one was saying anything to me. I was feeling much better physically, but sadness was creeping into my mind as I thought about Mama. I could not understand why Mama had been there with me and now she was gone.

Suddenly I noticed a stranger was in the room with me. He was standing up against the wall, and there I was with my chest uncovered and all exposed. This young man was just standing there looking at me.

Then he spoke. "Will you help me . . . please?"

I just stared at him, not saying a word, then grabbed my sheet and pulled it up over my chest. My first thought was that he must be lost. I thought to myself, "Why is he in here with me? Why doesn't he ask the nurse for help?" At first I didn't want to say anything, but he just kept standing there. Finally I asked one of the nurses that came in to check on me if he was lost or something.

The nurse said, "He? Who are you referring to Karen?"

"Over there . . . him," I said as I pointed at the wall where he was standing.

She looked at the wall and then back at me, "Karen I think you need to rest now . . . okay?"

I knew right then she couldn't see him, there was no doubt in my mind. I know the nurse thought that I had fallen off the turnip truck. She didn't say anything else to me after that and she left the room. I'm sure she thought that I had fallen off the turnip truck—or probably that I was hallucinating, I guess. "Yep . . . been there, done that already missy thank you very much," I thought to myself. The man never left the room, he just kept standing there looking at me.

Then Mama and Almeta appeared to me. Sis asked me if I would like to come home. Mama just gave Sis one of her *Hush-Up* looks. Then my daughter came rushing through the doorway, pushing the curtain aside. She was crying as she took my hand in hers and asked me what had happened. I told her about Mama coming into the bathroom and telling me how to breathe and about the man that was standing there in the room with us.

Kim was crying, "Mom, if you need to go with grandma . . . it's okay, you can go."

On the one hand I wanted to go with Mama and Sis, but on the other hand I needed to stay here. I felt I could make a difference in my daughter's life. For the first time, I knew I could help my child. I had to make a choice and the time was now. When I looked back at my little girl . . . now a woman, I knew I had to stay just a little longer; my work wasn't done yet. I told Kim I wanted to be here for her and my granddaughter, and for my son.

"But Mon," Kim said, as she held onto my hand tightly, "Don't you think you would be happier there instead of here? Think of how much you have missed grandma and Almeta." The tears rolled fast down her cheeks.

That's when I made up my mind, I was going to stay, there was still a lot to be done.

I heard Mama say, "Just do the work gal."

I knew I wanted to at least try. Kim looked at me so puzzled as she wiped away her tears.

All of a sudden I could feel a sensation like water running all over me. I was still holding onto Kim's hand. I sat up on the gurney table. "Kim, do you feel that? Can you hear the water?" I said. I could feel water running over my entire body and it was making a gurgling sound. Kim looked right at the sink and then looked back at me with a pale face.

"Noooo . . . ?" she said, her voice fading out as though she was unsure of herself.

I knew better, I know she heard it. As I sat there, I could hear in my mind two doctors talking in a room that was too far away to hear normally. They were down the hall from where I was at.

"Yes," I heard the voice say to the other doctor in an agreeing tone. "We both know what it looks like, but it's not in my medical text books and that is that! As far as I'm concerned, this is an anxiety attack; I'm not touching this." A few moments later the doctor walked into my room.

As he came toward me, I said, "So, you're gonna call this anxiety . . . huh?" He looked so surprised I thought that he was gonna drop everything that was in his hands. He didn't say anything, just looked down at the clipboard he was holding and signed my release papers.

Before he walked out of the room, he reached over and wiggled my big toe and said, "You can go home now . . . and take it easy, okay." And then he asked if I'd like to talk to someone from mental health.

"Sure, why not," I said feeling pretty low at that point. The doctor scooted out of the room quickly.

A few moments later there was another man that came in to see me. He was from the mental health department. He wanted to see if I felt like talking to him about how I was feeling, or maybe vent a little about Mama. "Sure, what does it matter now, you all think I'm nuttier than a fruit cake anyway," I said.

He patted my hand and said, "No one thinks that about you." Then he continued. "Grief does funny things to people. I am aware of the losses in your family, and I think it might help if you talked about it; don't you think so?"

"What can say to you to make you understand that my mother and sister *were here* with me! Right here in this room!" I asked.

He said, "But aren't they deceased Karen?"

"Yes, they are!" I answered back quickly. "They were here with me. I know they were! Not you or anyone else is going to make me think any different!"

"There, there now; don't get upset," he said to me, "Would you like me to write you a prescription? Some medication might help you feel better."

"I feel fine, thank you, and no, I don't need anything like that. I never have taken them before and I ain't gonna start now. I never did like taking stuff that made me feel goofy," I told him.

My daughter told me that I didn't have to be so abrupt with him, he was only inquiring about what my problems were and just wanted to be helpful.

I just sat there, thinking to myself, "They all think I've just lost it."

My eyes looked like I had been crying for a week. I had huge circles that ran all the way under my eyes and going deep into my cheeks. Then Nick came rushing into the room. He was crying as he told me how much he loved me and that I meant the world to him. He had been scared to death when he went into our apartment and saw all the stuff all over the floor where the paramedics had been working on me. I told him I was okay and that the doctor said I had an anxiety attack and that's all it was. His mouth dropped open and he said that was a bunch of bull, he didn't believe that for one minute. So, fourteen hours after I had been admitted, I was released to go home.

I was in a daze over everything that had happened. My legs were like Jello. My daughter borrowed a wheelchair, and she and Nick took me home. The ride home was very quiet; I was exhausted. All I wanted to do was just rest. Kim tried calling mental health to make an appointment for me. I heard her as she tried to explain to the lady what had happened. She wasn't having much luck; the lady seemed to not have much compassion for the situation.

Then Kim said sharply "No! She's never taken drugs of any kind, ever! Yes, I am positive!" she said. "No, I don't believe she needs that . . . Oh . . . just never mind," I heard her say as she hung up the phone. "I can't believe those people down there!" She looked angry. "I think she's the one that needs a shrink, Mom. She was not paying attention at all."

"Never mind, honey, I don't need their help. I just need to rest. I'll be better, I know I will. Don't you worry, okay?" I said trying to console her.

Kim was so frustrated. The woman she had talked to thought I was off my hat, that's all. By now I was getting pretty used to this kind of response. It really didn't matter at that point. "Mom, do you want to go in to talk to someone?" Kim asked.

"I'll take care of it babe, don't you worry," I told her.

My phone was ringing off the hook. Kim answered it. I heard her explain to one of my friends why I had missed meeting them that day. She was on the phone for the next little while. As Kim talked, I could hear her voice softening as she spoke. For the first time I heard her talk in a compassionate tone of voice about me. It had been very hard for her to go through all of this. I understood completely. And now she was being told by the people that were calling—total strangers to her, but people who I had previously sat with—how much I had helped them in their lives. I could tell by the look on her face as she talked to them that she was totally surprised. I had tried to tell her what I was able to do. I don't think she believed me, now she had no choice but to believe me.

After a little while she was ready to go home. "Mom are you going to be okay?" she asked.

"Sure. Go ahead and go home," I told her. After she left, I told Nick that we were not alone. The young man that I had seen standing in my hospital room was there with us—I didn't want to frighten Kim any more than she had been already so I hadn't said anything. He asked me who he was. "I don't know," I told him.

Nick just stood up and looked at the wall and started saying, "Let's leave her alone now okay; she has had enough for one day."

I cracked a smile at him because he was facing the wrong wall. "He's over there," I said as I pointed to the other wall. Then the man just dissipated, so I guess he heard Nick okay anyway. We went to bed, and Nick held me for the longest time. I laid there, exhausted from all that had happened. I thanked God for all my blessings. I asked Him to help me see what I needed to do next and to give me the strength to follow through.

An Unusual Message

A COUPLE OF DAYS LATER, THE PRAYER CIRCLE met again and I really felt the need to go. I needed to be there for the spiritual fulfillment that I had felt before. The group was glad to see me and that I was all right—they had heard that I had been in the hospital and they all showed their concern for me. This night, however, was different; there were many new people that had come. We all gathered in the living room just talking about one thing and another waiting for everyone to arrive. After a little while, it seemed everyone who was going to be there had arrived, so we went downstairs to the prayer room.

When I walked into the room, there was the same young man (in spirit) that had been in my hospital room. He was sending me a message; I could hear him as plain as day. I just headed for the table so I could sit down before I fell down.

"Tell her she's got the balls," he said.

Man, I didn't want to even listen to him. I was stunned by what I heard him say. I didn't say a word. I didn't let on that I knew he was even there. Nick had sat down beside me, we were holding hands.

"Are you okay?" he asked.

I didn't say anything, I just started squeezing his hand tighter and tighter.

"*Please,*" the young man said.

I still didn't say anything. As everyone all gathered around the table we all held hands and started to pray. There were many of us around that table, at least ten or twelve people. When it got to be my turn to pray, the young man spoke again.

"Please tell her . . . she's got the balls, Karen."

I was squeezing Nick's hand very tight. I knew he could tell that something was going on. I didn't know what to say.

"Please, tell her for me."

I kept my eyes shut. I wanted to say something but I wasn't sure what that would be. I couldn't say what he wanted me to say. I heard Angie asking me if someone was talking to me. "Ah . . . uh-huh," I said.

"Who is it?" she asked.

I shrugged my shoulders as if to say I didn't know. He started telling me that Angie was writing his name on paper. She had shown it to *his* sister who was sitting next to Angie at the other end of the table, which was eight feet or so away from where I was sitting. I saw his hand-written name in my mind. "Ted," I answered. I opened my eyes and he was standing behind a young woman.

"This is my little sister," he said, "We got along good and we were tight." Then Ted moved behind the lady that was at the head of the table. "She is my sister as well," he said, "Tell her to just let it go, it really doesn't matter anymore."

I told them what he said. When she heard my words, she had to leave the room; she was so overcome with emotion. It had to have been very hard for them to hear the words that were coming out of my mouth.

Angie said, "Just say the *exact words* that you hear Karen."

I had a hard time repeating Ted's remark about the balls, because he was directing me say it to an elderly lady that he said was his mother. I had a hard time explaining this one because of the way he was talking, so I chose to say something different than what he had said. I paused and said, "Oh he's saying something about basketballs." In my silence they knew I was communicating with this spirit.

"*No, No*," he said, "*Please tell her she's got the balls.*" Angie asked me again to use his words exactly.

Reluctantly I did.

The little old lady at the table started smiling from ear to ear. Through tears of joy she cried, "That's *my boy! Oh my God that's my boy!*"

He moved behind her and said, "*This is my mom, Karen. Please tell her I love her and that I'm okay.*" He told me that he had had a brain aneurysm and that was how he died a few months earlier. It was so sudden and unexpected. Some of the family had thought that his death was suspicious. He was just going in for a test, nothing more, and it all happened so quickly everyone was still in shock. He wanted to let his family know that he was all right. His older sister and he had had a disagreement and had not made up before his death. He wanted to tell her how much he loved her and that it was okay, he understood the stubbornness, it was a family trait that they had. He was finally able to tell his family what they had been trying to find out since his death. The message had been sent and received in the right way. He now was content and happy.

After a few minutes his mother came over and sat down beside me. She told me the story behind "the balls." He had given her some chocolate balls not long before his death, and told her she had the balls to just say no whenever she wanted to. She thanked me over and over many times for what I had done for them.

I didn't feel I had done anything. I was in a fog myself as to how this all had happened. I was so amazed by it, I could hardly believe it myself.

It was then that I realized that the room had pretty much cleared itself of all the people that had been there. I don't think they expected what they heard and witnessed that night. The others were very moved by it all. And me . . . I just shook my head in disbelief. I had never met this young man or known of him. It was overwhelming for me, and I'm sure it was for that family as well.

So the war between logic and spirituality continued for me, but now it had added more confusion. Nick said he didn't see anything in the prayer room, but he could feel a coolness in the air while we were talking. He said he wasn't spooked by the ordeal; but I thought he seemed to look a little pale.

An Enlightening Experience

THE NEXT DAY, WHEN NICK CAME IN FROM work, we started talking about what had happened at the prayer circle the night before. He said, "Karen, do you realize what you can do and the difference you can make? If you just pay attention, you will never have to worry about a roof over your head again."

I just looked at him; my mind was in a whirl. I was still in my own thoughts about the night before, I was so amazed at how it all had come together. "I don't understand what happened last night Nick, do you?"

"No, I've never seen anything like that before," he said. "But you need to do the best you can to let it work for you, Karen."

"But Nick I didn't learn this at a school, it's just there," I told him. "I feel so strange about all this. Did you see the way they all looked at me when we were going home? Maybe I shouldn't have said anything at all."

"Don't you think for a minute that what you told those people last night wasn't appreciated, Karen," he said. "Do you really think you would have *it* if you weren't meant to use *it*?"

"I don't know, Nick," I said. "This is pretty weird. I wonder why they (the spirits) are coming to me."

Nick went into the bedroom. I sat in the chair still in my own world thinking about it, over and over trying to make sense of it all in my mind. "Hey, Karen," Nick called out. "Come over and look at this, will ya." I got up and walked into the room. He had brought some maps of Utah home with him and had pinned an eight-foot map on the bedroom wall. "Neat huh!" he said, "I thought you could sit here on the side of the bed and see if you could find anything on the map. What do ya think?" He had even brought stickpins so I could mark out the places if I were to locate anything.

"And I thought I had seen it all," I thought to myself. I ended up looking at the map trying to pacify him by checking it out.

We ended up going to meet a man named Gary in Park City. Nick had told Gary what I was picking up from the maps. The man told us I had been right on many things. I felt like Nick and I needed to discuss this further, I didn't like the way I felt about the whole thing.

On the drive back to Salt Lake Nick began to tell me that people like me were in demand. "If you would just look at the whole picture," he said. I barked back at him angrily that I thought he was wrong. Back and forth we went for hours; even after we had made it back home, the argument went on over the do's and don'ts of our situation. I started having a hard time breathing because I was so upset. We both decided to shut-up.

I walked over to the oxygen concentrator machine that I'm hooked up to when I'm at home and turned the knob a couple of times so I could get more air. I had been so angry, I didn't realize just how much I had turned that sucker up. I couldn't catch my breath and it took quite a long time before I did. I was shaking bad and I wasn't sure what to expect next. Nick and I apologized to one another, we both agreed that we should just go to bed and sleep on it—both of us had forgotten that I had turned the air up on the concentrator.

I wasn't sure what time it was when a light woke me up from a sound sleep. At first I just kind of peeked through my eyes thinking, "What the heck is Nick doing up this late?" But this wasn't Nick. There in front of me was what appeared to be two balls of light floating at the top of the bedroom doorway. There was a third one, much bigger than the other two, it was as if it were peeking around the edge of the door about where the doorknob was. This ball of light was shinning into my eyes to wake me up.

At first I was startled, but almost as soon as I had seen them I felt that it would be okay. I realized this ball of energy was emitting a light in the darkest of the night. I got up out of the bed and walked into the front room where my oxygen concentrator was. One of the balls was releasing a light so bright that I could see the dial on the machine—it said five liters.

"Holly Mollie," I thought, "It's a wonder that I didn't turn into a flipping balloon!" I turned it back down to only two liters where it belonged.

The balls of light were still floating in mid-air. As I looked in wonder at what was taking place there in my front room, I realized that it was the middle of the night but I could see perfectly clear. "That's funny," I thought.

I needed glasses real bad back then. Under normal situations I couldn't see well at all, especially in the dark, but I sure could see this night. The balls were floating side by side, all three of them.

As I watched them in wonder, I could feel them as if they were pulsating. I had no fear in my heart at all, only love and an understanding that they loved me. Then they all moved to join each other in the center of the room. As I watched them, they appeared to shimmer and float effortlessly, glowing like soft gold and white silk drifting on a breeze. They looked so beautiful because of what they held inside of each of them.

They moved together to become one and at that moment they burst into a million tiny sparkles—like little flakes falling after they had been blown out of a firecracker. I sat down in my chair and started to cry. I didn't know what or who they were, but I felt like they had saved me in some way. time

I felt in my heart that those three balls of energy had been Mama, my Sis Aleta, and Daddy. I'm just sure of it. My thought back then was that it was gonna take time to get used to things like this happening to me. To this day, I know in my mind it was real; it wasn't a dream of any kind. I never realized that you could miss family so much as I was missing them. I knew that I would see them again, there was no doubt in my mind about that. I think they were there to give me support in what I believed in and the strength to endure.

The next morning I told Nick what I had seen. He just lifted his eyebrows and suggested that I should talk to my friends at the prayer group about it. "Maybe Angie or Kathy would understand it," he said.

"How do you explain floating bubbles?" I asked him.

"I don't know, Karen," he said, "How do you explain a lot of what goes on these days?"

As I thought about this experience, I remembered seeing others like that on the other side, but that was a long time ago when my home was in another place, the place where we all come from. And then, when I had my accident, I had seen others like that, and then I saw the Guardian. I knew at that time they were people just like me, but in a different form, and here they look like pure energy. I don't know how I knew that, I just did.

Well, little by little more people came my way. I kept telling my story to anyone that wanted to hear it. I think Nick was trying to help, but his intentions always looked different to me somehow; he seemed to be focused on the lime-light. He told me that he felt that I deserved a better life than what I had and he thought I should listen to him more often. I was so mixed up, I really didn't know what to do, so I let him guide my way. We talked a lot back then about so many things. He told me he thought that I got the 'short end of the stick,' as he put it.

I know there were times that it scared the heck out of him, although he would never admit to it. I remember many times when he would come home and go into a room that we had not been in all day and the lights would come on without his help. "H-e-l-l-o-! They're here again," he would say, as he made an abrupt U-turn and come back out of the room.

It happened to me all day long when Nick was at work so I was getting used to it. Sometimes we would be making dinner and you could smell perfume the same perfume as my Mama used to wear coming out of the hallway. Or there would be a knock on our door and no one would be there when you opened it up. Most of the time I could sense others there; the spirits would tell me who they were and who they needed to talk to, or they would tell me I needed to see someone and give someone a message from the other side.

Nick was a good listener and he helped me figure it out. Both of us were having a tug of war with our emotions back then. He kept on trying to tell everyone he could about me. At times I felt like a bag of groceries, like I needed to feed everyone that came in contact with me. Nick and I had had our times; that's for sure. I shared so much of myself with him and he got to know me better than anyone had in my whole life. He really tried to take the fear out of all the strange things that were going on back then.

Special Thought and Prayers

M̲Y̲ ̲F̲R̲I̲E̲N̲D̲ ̲K̲A̲T̲H̲Y̲ asked if I would come over to her house and tell my near death story to some of her friends. I agreed and I was ready to go, but it got too cold for me outside. So I called her and asked if they would come over to our little apartment instead. They all came. There were eight of them and myself. We all squeezed into that little front room and started talking. Hours later, everyone was moved by what they had heard. They asked me questions about many different things. I was amazed that I was able to have a response to all of their questions, because they asked so many different things.

One of the gentlemen that had come that night brought his wife along, too. I was aware she was in the nursing field even though she had not told me so. When I asked her if she liked being a nurse, she just kind of laughed—I caught her off guard when I told her what she did for a living. Her husband was an American Indian and he asked me questions regarding his background and heritage.

As I began to feel Spirit coming closer to me, I started talking to a wonderful (spirit) woman who we found out was his grandmother. I could see this lady in my mind's eye. She expressed how she felt about his life and what he was doing with it. She remarked about the cleansing and sweating ceremony. She also mentioned the fact that he was building a log cabin. I had never previously met this man and his wife or known anything about them. He gave me a feather that I still have to this day and he made a figurine for me of a head with a face on it; he said he thought it was a spirit guide that followed me.

A few years later he had a ceremony to bless the cabin that he had built with his own hands. He gave it a name when it was finished and then he offered it to the Great Spirit. He felt that Spirit had lead him to build this place as a retreat for others to go to when they wanted or needed to dwell with the Great One. He offered it to me to use for future retreats and meetings with groups of people that needed to get away from the everyday hustle and bustle.

We talked about many things that night, and covered a lot of territory in a short matter of time. The people that had come to talk and listen were from different walks of life. One of the ladies had sat very quietly between others on the couch never saying a word. She was listening intently to everything that was being said. I asked her if she was all right and she said, "Yes."

I looked deeply at her and said, "Well that's funny, because my hip is killing me right now and I thought it was you that I was feeling."

Her mouth fell open and she said, "Well you're right, my hip *is* hurting, how did you know that?"

"I don't know," I said. "This happens a lot these days."

It got pretty late and so we had to stop the meeting. Everyone was yawning and showing signs of being tired, but none of us really wanted to stop talking. They all asked if we could meet again. "Sure, let's do it," I said. So we made a date to go over at Kathy's house the following month. That evening turned out to be so incredible. On one hand it was unbelievable, and on the other it was very incredible because what was taking place was very real. I didn't know the people that were coming so I didn't know what to expect. I had never done this before. It was fun but a little different, I'll tell ya.

Nick was so surprised when he got home from work that night. He thought that everyone would be gone, not just getting ready to go. He got into a conversation with the Indian man because he liked the culture. Nick just shook his head and said, "There is something strange about this gal but it works!... At least she talks about positive things," he added. It was as if he was very proud of what I could do. Then he looked at me and said, "You look tired Karen."

Normally I would have been very tired and needed my rest, but I felt like I could have talked all night. There have been many times when I wouldn't know when to shut up. It's as if I need to tell all I can while I can. I want to tell people that there so much more than we have seen or are aware of out there.

Although I have tried to get used to being this way, it still takes a lot out of me physically. I continue to talk to people, I want to try and help them. When I feel that there is something I can say to an individual, I've found that a little kindness really does make the difference. I wish I had all the answers, but I don't. But I think I have a better way of seeing things now than I ever did before. I'll share it until the day I leave this place. It's as simple as taking a breath—if we just allow it, that is.

After every meeting people would ask if I would have another. I would try to do one every month after that for over a year and new people always came. I remembered Angie saying, "You won't have to worry about the people showing up, Karen; spirit will take care of that." She said it would be like a match in dry brush, and it has been just like that. I only had the one group meeting at our apartment. After that first meeting, we moved it to Kathy's place for more room. The meetings to come were incredible. It was so amazing to see it all come together.

The Indian man came to another meeting and offered to play a flute he had made with his own hands. Many spirits came to help that night. While this was going on, the strangest thing happened to me, right there in front of everyone else to see. Nick had earlier surprised me with a cute pair of stud earrings and I was wearing them that night. When I started talking to the people, the dad gum earrings literally flew out of my ears, just like they had been shot out of a gun.

Nick just looked at me and said, "What was that? What was that sound?"

I grabbed both my ears and both of my earrings were gone. "My earrings just fell out of both my ears, can you believe that?" I reached up and touched my ears again; sure enough both earrings were gone! I must have looked pretty silly, 'cause my mouth was wide open with disbelief.

"What the heck caused that to happen?" I asked. All I had done was lower my head getting ready to talk to spirit. We all had been just sitting there in the front room. I didn't know what to expect next and nether did anyone else.

Nick looked back at me in disbelief, then asked for everyone to please stay seated so he could look for my earrings. One of them was across the room by the sliding glass doors and the other was under the table next to me—everybody in the room heard it when it hit the table. I stopped wearing earrings for a few years after that.

The group asked me many questions about what I thought was going to happen to other people in the world. Or they would ask me about other states or countries, places I had never seen much less known about. They wanted to know my thoughts on many things. Most of the time it was like reading a book in my head, if that makes any sense to you.

What was hard on me, was when I saw bad things taking place. I have found there is a large responsibility that goes with this "war of the minds," as I call it. I don't tell people the frightening things that I see. I try to stay positive instead. Some things are funny and lighthearted while some are not. My sense was *balance within*. When I see people hurting I feel so helpless. People will say things to me like, "Do you realize how lucky you are?" or, "Have you gone to Las Vegas yet?" and, "You must have total happiness, now that you know where you are going."

Nick and I were talking one evening about all that was going on with me. "What if I'm wrong Nick?" I said. "What if . . ."

He cut me off. "Karen you can 'what if' yourself to death if you try hard enough. Don't worry about it; can't you see the bigger picture here?"

"Well, I can't help it, that's the way I feel," I said. I just couldn't believe all that was going on.

"Karen," he continued, "I don't think you have even scratched the surface yet."

Sharing with Others at IANDS

WHEN I FIRST FOUND OUT THAT THERE WERE others like myself right here in Salt Lake City, it made me feel a lot better. For a long time I felt like I was the only one in the world that was like this. I found comfort in the fact that others had similar experiences. It's hard when you don't fit in anywhere. When you feel like an oddball and everyone thinks you have stepped off the deep end.

It had been so hard for me to accept what had happened along with all the changes that I had made in my life. I wondered if any of the others had had such a change in their lives or behavior, or if their experiences had affected them in a different way; I wanted to find out.

When I talked with the president of IANDS (International Association of Near Death Studies) it was over the phone in the fall of 1997. At their meetings, people like myself talk and hash over their experiences; and no one there thinks you're weird. Salt Lake City, to my understanding, has the largest Near Death Experience (NDE) chapter in the world, but I had never heard about them until I got this call.

I knew that this was someone that was really interested in the truth, not just someone trying to pick my brain. We talked for quite some time on the phone, he was very reassuring. He understood exactly how I was feeling. It felt so good to hear reassurance from someone else that had an experience as unusual and as hard to explain as mine has been.

I knew that he had had an experience different than my own, but I didn't intrude or ask. It felt so good to talk to him about what had happened to me. I was somewhat surprised when he shared that others had come back from death with all the same confusion and bewilderment. I wouldn't wish what has happened to me on anyone—I'll tell ya . . . it was hell. All the *adjustments*, as I call it, have been difficult, to say the least; nothing has been the same for me. I asked him if everyone that he knew was like that. He simply said that there have been many who have said that their experience had completely changed their lives in one way or another. Boy I could understand what he was saying there. He asked me if I would give a lecture on my near death experience. I had been ill for so long, I didn't have the strength. I told him that as soon as I got better, I would love to. I thanked him for his time and for inviting me to IANDS.

He wasn't aware how sick I had been. I'd had bronchitis for several weeks, and actually thought that I was gonna die. I only had about nineteen percent total lung capacity left since the accident., so I have to be very careful; even the common cold can knock my socks off. This sickness had gotten the better part of me. I was tired of putting it off, so I finally decided to take things into my own hands and called a local funeral director. He came to my house and sat with me. We drew up the necessary papers to take care of things when the time came.

Nick got so angry at me for thinking that way. I told him I felt it was an important thing for me to do under the circumstances. I was awfully weak; I felt that I could be leaving at any time. I was so sick I couldn't bathe myself or wash my hair, I was in pretty sad shape. I couldn't even cut my food at one point, I just didn't have enough strength in my body to do a simple task.

A year later I was still here, still recuperating from the bronchitis that I had had. My doctor said I was very lucky. I just shook my head. "I guess I'm not done yet, huh." I told him.

The doctor just smiled at me. "Evidently not," he said with a twinkle in his eye. He had me on medications and other antibiotics off and on to try and heal my poor lungs.

I was still trying to talk to as many people as I could. I don't know how I was able to do it back then. I decided that I needed to start telling people, "If you are sick, I can't see ya." I had to stick to my guns on that one, otherwise I wouldn't be here to help them or anyone else.

One evening, about a year after our initial conversation, I talked to the president of IANDS again. I was much better than I had been when I spoke to him the year before, and many more things had changed for me. So when he asked me again if I would speak at IANDS, I accepted the invitation gladly. I had never felt so comfortable before. I was excited to be able to tell my experience to people that cared and shared a common interest.

I was nervous about speaking in front of so many

people. I had never been to anything like this before so I didn't know what to expect. When I got there that night, I sat down trying to catch my breath. The evening started with a very important note of information to us all. The President of IANDS mentioned the fact that people would see us NDE's as different and maybe even *saintly*.

"Boy," I thought to myself, "If these fools only knew all the bones in my closet, they wouldn't be thinking like that about *me,* that's for sure!"

Then he introduced me and I stood up, thinking to myself "This is what I've needed to do since I came back!" All I ever wanted was to tell someone that would listen and try to understand me. For a long time I thought that I was the only one who had endured something so astounding; I had been living in my own world until now. Something so incredibly wonderful had taken place for me and I wasn't the only one; I wasn't alone after all.

I started to tell my story and as I looked into the eyes of the people, I could tell the ones that had had their own experience. Their tears came from a very deep place inside of them. These were not sad tears—they were tender and loving, bringing back to their minds a moment that they had seen and felt on their own journey, remembering their own experience. I could see it in their eyes and on their faces.

As I spoke to them, I noticed they had a look about them. So deep was their stare, then they would gently nod their heads to agree with me, as if they had seen or felt the same thing I had. It was such a treat to hear the comments and questions from the audience. One lady raised her hand and she spoke softly but clearly. "Do you think you have been to heaven?"

"Well sugar," I said, "I truly don't know if it was heaven or not that I saw, but it would be okay with me if it wasn't! I have always hoped and prayed for at least two blades of grass in the lower forty—if I made it, that is—and I wouldn't mind going back to wherever I had been, that's for sure." They all just laughed at me.

Another person raised her hand and simply said, "You know Karen those balls that you were talking about . . ."

"Yes," I said.

"I call them *floating bubbles*; they just seemed to float so easily and without effort didn't they?"

I thought that was a much better description than "floating balls." I felt a great relief to know someone else had seen them as well. Then I was asked if I saw the tunnel. "No," I answered, "I don't remember a tunnel . . . only the place I had been. It was as if I were speeding through a galaxy of some kind. I saw the most beautiful things, like different dimensions or galaxies. It was all around me but it didn't look like any kind of a tunnel or walls. It was very vast and the colors were magnificent."

Another lady raised her hand and asked me about the music I had heard. "Well the music seemed to be faint, like it was way, way off in the background. It was like voices singing notes only, no words, just the chords. Precious voices that were beautifully singing in this wondrous place," I said.

I was also asked if I saw God. "No . . . I didn't, but I *felt* Him; I knew He was there with while I was there with the Guardian."

I was asked if the Guardian was Jesus. "When I think of Him my heart swells with love and admiration for what He (the Guardian) showed me and his love for me," I said. "In all honesty . . . I don't know who He was, but I love Him and He loved me. That's why I call him the Guardian."

I was asked if I hurt anywhere physically when I saw things from that dimension. "No, I did not," I answered. "It was as if I had no connection to emotion; at one point, it was as if I was an observer only."

I enjoyed the fact that people accepted what I had become and where I had been. It had been very hard for me for a long time to accept how I came back. I don't want people to think that I'm this "wonder woman," not at all. I just want to share my story. It has taught me a great deal, and if it can bring any peace to someone's troubled world, than I have done what I was intended to do.

The Guardian had asked me if I had the chance to change anything would I? And I meant what I said when I told Him that I would help people whenever I could, however I could, for whatever reason as long as it was for the good of mankind and for God's sake. I guess I loaded my bucket pretty darn good, I'd say.

I noticed that one of the ladies in the front row was listening intently. She had experienced something, I could see such sadness in her eyes. As I talked about the other side, her eyes would flood up with the memory of her own experience. It was a bittersweet feeling, you could tell. I try to make eye contact as much as possible when I'm talking to people, I need to look at them.

There was a very special woman that I met at IANDS, named MaryAnn. She had a neat sense of humor and is one nice gal. She asked me if I would to talk to her daughter sometime. "You just tell me when, I'd be more than happy to," I told her. MaryAnn is such a sweet gal and my heartstrings were definitely being pulled. All she had been through and what she was gonna go through again soon made me feel so bad for her. Although she had not told me about her personal life, there was much that I could see.

When I was finished speaking Nick reminded me that it was time to go because it was time for my medication treatments. He was trying to push the people aside that were encircling me so he could get me out of the building.

All I could say was, "I'm sorry, I have to go." They were trying so hard to get just one more question asked. Just one more question. People have no idea how many times I've heard that statement, just one more question. How I wished that there were more hours in the day so I could help them all.

I never even got a chance to thank the President of IANDS—there was a lady from one of the local newspapers that had his attention. I was only able to make eye contact with him just as I was going out the door, we nodded our many ways, but I felt like I had been through the wringer physically and emotionally.

A Time To Let Go

NICK AND I HAD CHANGED IN SO MANY WAYS. He wanted me to go as far as I could with my gifts, and his thoughts of marketing me seemed to take priority. I tried to explain to him how I felt about "soap box standing," as I call it.

My lawsuit over the accident had started in 1994 and had been going on for well over two years. Nick and I had been together for almost a year when the lawsuit was thrown out.

I was devastated for many reasons. I had told Nick from the beginning that I didn't think the suit would go anywhere, but I had hoped that the truth would prevail. The test I had taken nine months after the accident had occurred would have proved that there was indeed foreign matter inside both of my lungs, but the insurance doctors had misplaced the test. It was the only piece of evidence that I had that would help me prove my case. After hearing the evidence that was on hand, they ended up calling it a pre-existing condition.

Without the missing CT test, I didn't have a chance. I had never been treated for the sickness that they had diagnosed me with. Yes, I had admitted to being a smoker, but I had quit a few years prior to the accident. I had thought and felt that I had been in great shape. I had been a truck driver (eighteen wheelers) prior to moving to Utah,and was required to have a health check up every two years by law in order to drive legally. Not one doctor ever said anything to me of a lung problem until the accident at the laundromat. The CT scan had conveniently gone missing after the insurance doctors saw it. That was the only piece of evidence that could prove my case. I had no one on my side—not even my lawyer. I've heard of blind justice before, but this was more than I could stand.

While Barbara was on the witness stand, I couldn't help how I felt at that moment. I stared at her as she told this tall tale about how she depicted it all to really be, completely discrediting me, and I blurted out. "God help you!"

The Workman's Compensation Court dismissed my suit moments later and I walked out of that court room feeling more alone than I ever had in my life. I wondered why these people were so set against believing the truth. I was in a daze. It was bad enough having to push an oxygen tank around, but to be thought of in this manner was more than I could bear. I guess they thought it was all for show. I felt like I finally hit the bottom. There was nowhere else for me to go. When I got home that day I cried for hours. There was nothing left to do or say.

When Nick came home I told him what had happened. I couldn't figure out why in the world I just couldn't die and get it over with. Why should I have to come back here to this? At least when I was on the other side I was loved and in peace. This physical life was the opposite of everything that I had been shown when I was there. Nick begged me to not talk like that, he tried consoling me. I cried so hard, not because I lost the case but because no one believed me or took the time to go over everything to give me a fair shake.

It was several days before I could even sleep because it was eating me up so bad. When you have fought the war and lost the battle there is nothing else you can do . . . but let it go.

I had hoped that the truth of the chemicals would be found out, but they were never even mentioned. I had hoped that others might not have to go through what I had to and lose as deeply as I had. Incidentally, two weeks after my case had been dismissed, I mysteriously received the missing C.T. scan in the mail with no return address. Now it had no value in proving anything because once a case has been dismissed, you can't go back.

Nick was shocked and let down. Like so many others, he thought I would receive some compensation for my accident and my loss. He was angry and he acted different for several days afterwards. Over the next few weeks the mood sure changed between Nick and I. Nick wasn't even acting like his normal self anymore. It was as if there wasn't enough money to do anything. Money seemed to be the topic of everything we talked about these days. We had talked about buying our own home someday; we even looked at several that he found. At one time he had shared his dream about us traveling to different places together. He had wanted to just quit his job and take care of me after everything was settled.

Now it seemed like everything had changed. He quit his driving job and went to work for a construction company, hoping to make better money. He had been promised that he would be taught how to operate a compactor, but as it turned out, they put him in a ditch, digging holes. It was killing him to have to work this way. He came home just dragging and pretty grumpy. I knew he couldn't last much longer at this pace. He was only fifty one years old, but this was too hard on him and we both knew it.

Weeks later he tried to get me to go south, to the Utah Desert to look for treasure there. "At least it was a lower elevation," he said. Again I refused. I had my near death experience for a reason, and in my heart I knew that my gifts were not to be used in that manner. He told me that I was being very selfish. Shortly after that we separated.

I have learned a lot about integrity and honesty; I think the experience alone has helped me to understand and find compassion for everyone . . . even Nick. It was hard at first letting go of him because we had shared so much together in so many ways in the three and a half years we were together. He was there for me when no one else was. He went on with his new life and so did I. Thank God for my friends, my gifts and a new year in front of me.

My First Memories

I BEGAN TO RECALL MEMORIES OF MY CHILD-hood, and instances in my life when I had some extraordinary things happen to me . . .

A Near Fatal Decision

It was summer time. I was outside on the front porch at my Gramma's house with my cousin Dottie. Mama walked outside and headed for the car as she hollered at us, "Come on you two, get in the car, let's go." Dottie and I raced to see who could be the first one to reach the car. Even though she was 15 years old and I was only three and a half, I still beat her to the car. We jumped inside and headed into town.

Mama had to pick up a few things, so she went to the five-and-dime store. We were excited because Mama let us go get an ice cream cone at Gramma and Grandpa's restaurant across the street. "I'll meet you kids out-side in front of the store in a little bit, okay," Mama said.

Dottie grabbed my hand as we climbed out of the car and we went inside to get an ice cream cone. Gramma was happy to see us, and she gave us each an extra scoop of ice cream on our cones. Dottie and I thanked Gramma and went outside to wait for Mama. In a few minutes I saw her come out of the store across the street.

Dottie and I had been holding hands until I saw Mama. I jerked loose from her and took off across the street. Mama saw me and started screaming, "Stop, Stop," as she watched a car coming straight toward me. I was running toward her, and then I saw a beautiful soft white light glowing in front of me and an unfamiliar woman holding her arms out to me. I went into her arms without even a second thought.

"It's okay little one, everything will be all right," she said. I felt so good in her arms as she looked at me with such deep compassion.

Then the moment was broken, and I heard Mama's voice screaming out my name. I looked over and saw Mama, but the angel lady was gone. Mama knelt beside me gathering me up in her arms, crying hysterically.

I told Mama over and over about the pretty angel lady. "Where did she go Mama?" I cried.

Mama just kept rubbing my head, and telling me that I would be all right. I guess she thought that I was knocked silly

The driver of the car that had hit me (a 1950 Buick) was frantic and crying, "I'm so sorry, it all happened so fast. I didn't even see her. She just ran right out in front of me and I couldn't stop. Oh God I am so sorry," he kept saying over and over.

Mama sat me in her car, on the seat next to her, and said "Let's get her to the hospital." Mama's hands were shaking as she clutched the steering wheel, and she was crying, she was so upset. I kept trying to tell her about the lady that held me in the street. I think Mama thought I was hurt pretty bad. I scared the stuffing right out of her that was for sure. She thought I must have head injuries saying, "It's all right now Sugar, we'll be at the hospital in a minute. You'll be just fine."

When we arrived at the hospital, Mama was sure in a hurry to get me inside. She carried me in and Dottie followed us like a little shadow behind Mama. The nurse immediately took me and Mama into a room. Mama began to tell the doctor how I had run right out into the street and how the car had hit me and dragged me maybe 20 feet or so, on the front bumper. She thought she had lost me forever.

I just wanted to know where the angel lady was.

The emergency room doctor ordered x-rays. He checked me out from head to toe. I heard him tell Mama he couldn't believe it. "She's one lucky child! It's a miracle that she wasn't killed. I can't believe there are no broken bones, not even bruises, not even a scratch on her," he said. Then he gave me a sucker and patted me up and we headed back to Gramma's house. Dottie sat close to me all the way home, holding my hand so tight.

When we got to the house Mama carried me inside. She rubbed the top of me head, sat me down on the couch in the living room, and proceeded to tell me how the cow ate the cabbage! As she was shaking her finger at me she said, "Don't you ever do something like that again! Do you hear me? You scared the stuffing right out of me Karen. You a-l-w-a-y-s hold hands and look both ways before you cross a street! Do you understand what I'm telling you?"

"Yes ma'am," I answered her. I thought she was gonna warm my tail up for sure for scaring her so bad. Mama had never talked to me like that before, and she never talked about the angel lady that had saved me that day. But I never forgot her! I think, deep down inside, Mama knew that I had been saved by the angel lady.

My First Recognition of Their Presence

(Pre-existence)

I was about four years old when my family moved from Jamestown, California to Alameda, California. He promised it would be for just a short while, because we were country people not city folks. "There aren't so many people up in the hills," he said.

I was missing my grandparents pretty bad, and I stuck like glue to Mama's side. My grandparents had owned a restaurant In Jamestown, and I sure missed seeing them and getting free ice cream cones.

I didn't know at the time that I was different. I would find this out much later in life. I didn't realize that most of the friends I had as a young child were spirits. They (the spirits) came into my life at a young age, maybe about three years of age, I guess.

Mama always thought that I just had a vivid imagination. She walked into my bedroom one day to put some laundry away and heard me talking. "Who ya talking to kiddo? Are you playing house?" she asked.

"No, I'm talking to my friend," I said. Then I started telling Mama about her.

"H-E-R?" Mama asked. "Uh-huh," I said.

Mama listened to me for a little bit and then picked me up off the floor. Both her hands went under my arms and she sat me in the middle of my bed. Shaking her pointed finger at me with one hand and the other hand on her hip, she told me, "Quit talking like that right this minute, not another word! You better think about them lies, little lady, you know what happened to that little boy that lied don't cha'?"

All I could think about was the story of the little boy that cried wolf—I thought that wolf was gonna chew me up! And Pinocchio—his nose turned to wood! I held my nose for a long, long time not knowing what was gonna happen first!

Mama tried to make me admit that I was fibbing, but I wasn't gonna have my nose turn to wood. "You ought to be ashamed of yourself for talking like that Karen," she said. "I'm gonna tell your Daddy when he comes home! You know what happened to Pinocchio when he told all them lies. You want a snoot like that? Well do ya?" she continued.

I was in double-deep doo-doo again, and all I did was answer Mama's question.

"You just keep it up gal, 'cause that's what's gonna happen to you. You know how ugly you would be with a nose like that on your face? I sure wouldn't want to look like that, I'll tell ya."

I was so afraid that something was gonna happen, but nothing ever did. I knew I wasn't lying to Mama, but she didn't know that. Sometimes I felt like Mama thought I was not in my right mind. I was always getting myself in some kind of trouble with her.

Our neighbor's husband was in the Navy. One day he needed a ride back to his ship, so Mama offered to give him a ride. Almeta, my older sister, was in school. I was about four (I wasn't going to school yet) so I got to go along. Mama was telling him that she and Daddy had been married for nine years.

Then I piped up, saying, "Yeah that's right, 'cause I was there, too . . . it was in 1944, huh Mama?"

I was so proud I could remember. It was so clear in my mind, I could recall everything about my parents' marriage at that moment. I told the neighbor man how pretty Mama looked in her black skirt and her pretty checkered suit top, and the pretty flowers that were pinned to her shoulder.

Mama was shocked to hear me say that. She glared at me in her rear view mirror. "Karen, you shut your mouth up this minute . . . young lady you're gonna get it!" she hollered.

"But Mama you know that's right, 'cause you got mad at Daddy for putting a hole in your jacket when he pinned your flowers on, and that upset you 'cause it was the only nice outfit you owned," I said.

As I was talking, Mama's face got redder and redder. Mama was horrified to hear the words that were pouring out of my mouth. It's a wonder poor Mama didn't drive off the road. She just about broke her neck. Whipping her head around glaring at me in disbelief at what I was saying. "Karen, I ought to slap the stuffing out of you for lying like that," she yelled.

"But Mama, you know I was there. We were in Mr. JP's office (Justice of the Peace) that day when you and Daddy got married. I remember it," I said. "Don't you remember Mama?"

By now Mama was shooting daggers at me in the rear view mirror with her eyes! "Karen, what has gotten into you? You know that's a lie," she said. Her voice was breaking, 'cause she was so embarrassed and angry at what I was implying.

I wasn't aware of how I was making her appear in that man's eyes—I was too young to know or understand. I just knew I could remember. But no matter how much I tried to help Mama remember, I couldn't. She was pretty upset with me—I knew that much for sure! But Mama couldn't explain how I knew what I did.

As usual the subject was just dropped and not talked about. I would either get my butt warmed up for exaggerating or sent to my room to think about what I was doing wrong. We really never put it together and as the years went by . . . I just thought that I was a good guesser.

❋

Meeting My Angel

More memories continued to come to mind as I recalled another incident when I was about six or seven years-old. Juanita was a short lady that loved children of all ages. She had dark brown hair with a lot of gray mixed in. she was heavyset, but it didn't slow her down a bit. I remember her Nash Rambler station wagon. She would pick all of us kids up from school. She had a set of twins that were a year older than I was. Juanita had a big heart and truly loved people. She would sing songs like *Sink the Bismarck, the Titanic* and many others. She was a fun and loving woman!

One day our two families went to a place called Jenny Lind Creek for the day to swim and to have a picnic. The creek was surrounded by forest and sand mixed with large, smooth, round rocks. The water was colder than a well-diggers belly button 'cause it was melted snow that was coming out of the Mokelumne Hills, but on hot summer days that made it real nice. Looking out across the water in the deeper spots you could see the swells and swirls moving around and around on top of the water.

Mama said, "Those are undertows, and if you get caught in them, they will suck you under." I didn't know how to swim, so Mama told me that I couldn't go into the water, I was only allowed to play in the shallow part of the water near the shore.

I had found an old paper cup and started looking for pollywogs. There were lots of them, but they were pretty fast and hard to catch. The creek was really quite wide, so I could go out about 15 feet or so before it dropped off into the deep part. The water was only up to my knees. I hadn't noticed I was getting closer and closer to the other kids that were swimming. I was too engrossed in what I was doing (looking for my pollywogs).

I wasn't paying attention to just how far out I was going, when all of a sudden I fell straight down into the deep water. The undertow sucked me way down and it was pushing me downstream. It was as if I had stepped into a big hole with no bottom. The cup slipped out of my hand and I felt myself going deeper and deeper into the water. The water was swirling around me as though I were caught in a whirlwind. I felt like there was something that had a hold of me and it was pulling me down faster and faster. I was choking and kicking and waving my arms trying to get back to the top of the water, but the more I fought it, the more it took me down.

All of a sudden I could hear some kind of music. I felt a tingling sensation and *there she was again* . . . the beautiful angel lady that had helped me before, when the car had hit me. I could feel her arms around me and I wasn't afraid at all. It felt good with her there with me. I felt warm and comforted as I felt her love. All of the fear inside of me stopped and I quit struggling and fighting the water.

Juanita's son was one of the kids that was out in the deep part swimming. He had seen me go under and not come up. He swam hard to where he had last seen me go down in the water and dove deep for me three times. Later he tried to explain what had happened. He said that he saw something swirling around in the water and thought it was my hair but he was unsure, 'cause there was this green stuff that floated through the water making it hard to see. He grabbed at it, but it wasn't me! Then he saw some blonde hair and it was moving fast downward and kind of floating sideways with the current, he knew it had to be me. On his third attempt, he knew if he didn't get me it would be too late. Swirling around in a circle, he made a grab for the blonde hair. He pulled hard on my hair trying to get me to the top of the water.

By the time I reached the top I wasn't moving. He pulled me out of the water and laid me on the ground and started pushing on my back. I started choking and hacking and water started coming out of my nose and mouth at the same time, and the angel lady was gone. I told Mama about her as she was trying to hug the fear away from me, and then she started crying. She just hugged me and said, "You'll be all right but no more water for you young lady, not until you learn how to swim and that's that!" Juanita said she thought I must be part cat with nine lives.

Unexplainable, Remarkable Things

WITH THE PERMISSION OF THOSE INCLUDED in this section, I wish to share these sessions with you because I believe within each one there is a lesson for us all.

✳

A gentlemen once asked, "When you talk to people from the other side, do you see them as they were physically or are they different?"

I explained to him in the best manner that I could and used these examples:

The night Mama died, when I saw her standing in the middle of the road, she still looked the same to me. But she was wearing an aqua aand green night gown that I had never seen before. I found out later, from my kid sister, that Mama had died in that very gown. My sister had bought it for her the day she went into the hospital.

✳

The young man that I saw standing in the emergency room with me appeared to be a normal physical person, he didn't look different in any way. I had no idea who he was until he explained himself to me at the Prayer Circle. When his Mother showed me a picture of her son, it was the same young man I had described seeing. However, thinking back, I cannot remember seeing him from the waist down.

※

When I had my near death experience, I saw spheres of light that looked like balls of pure energy. They were passing by me at an incredible speed. However, I knew they were people but in different forms. They appeared to look like round balls of soft glowing gold, illuminating light; not solid, they were pulsating, as we are now. I know that sounds weird, but that's the only way I know how to explain it. The night that the three balls came to me in my bedroom, I have always felt they were my mother, father, and sister.

※

Sometimes when I sit close to people that are sick they have a soft, kind of blue-cast light that glows around their physical bodies. Others seem to have a soft, yet low, golden glow that circles around their entire body. When this happens, I normally can tell what kind of sickness they are dealing with. But everyone is different, and no two people have looked the same.

When I close my eyes and focus my thoughts on a person or name, most of the time I can see a face in my mind's eye. I call it "my Kodak moment." I see pictures of people that I have never known and have been able to talk in great depth with their families. They have come to me in many ways throughout the years. I can't explain why it happens this way. I just ask God to make it clear in my mind so that I can explain what I am seeing. I try not to go into negativity. I might see what I think is gonna happen, but I don't like to tell people the bad stuff.

✻

A lady named Claire once came to visit me, and as we began to talk, suddenly (in my mind) I could see an accident unfold right in front of my eyes. I couldn't see both of the cars, but I knew Claire was involved. I could see street sign—it said "Bangerter Highway" which is a local freeway that runs through town. I felt this accident was definitely gonna happen, and I wanted to stop it from happening if I could. As it all played out in my mind, I didn't say a word about what I was viewing. I just asked her to please stay away from Bangerter Highway for at least three to six weeks.

"R-e-a-l-l-y . . . Why?" she asked.

"Well I'm curious," I said, "Do you own a white Ford with the right front fender crunched up that has spray painted words on the side that reads "OUCH"?

"NO!," she answered. I could tell I had sort of offended her. Well I didn't want to explain all that I had seen, so again I asked her to avoid this highway for a few weeks and she should be fine. She kind of laughed a little and said, "Okay, I guess I can do that."

Well, one day my phone rang and this excited voice came over the line. "Karen?" she said. "This is Claire. Do you remember the lady you told to stay off of Bangerter Highway?"

"Yeah Sugar, go on, how can I help you?" I said. I could tell she was pretty shook up.

"Karen, you're not going to believe what happened! My sister came over to my house today to give me a ride in her brand new little convertible, so we took off for a spin. She pulled out across Bangerter Highway and this car . . . this car came out of nowhere and hit us on the driver's side. They said that my sister's arm and collarbone were broken. I hit my head on the glass and got a mild concussion."

"I am so sorry," I told her.

"Karen, it was a white car and the fender was spray painted 'OUCH!,' can you believe it? The kid had no insurance."

I had not explained anything about the accident that I had seen in my mind's eye. I had just hoped that I could detour this accident from happening. I guess that some things are meant to just be . . . go figure.

✳

One day I was at an arts and craft store. A lady was behind the counter and I could feel that she was in a lot of pain. I knew she had a bad toothache. It was a real butt kicker.

"Wow," I said, "You got a bad one going on huh?"

"Yeah I sure do, it really hurts," she said.

So I asked her if I could touch her face with my hands and maybe the pain might just go away.

She looked at me kind of funny, paused for a moment, then she said, "Okay, I don't have anything to lose."

When I took my hands away from her face, her mouth dropped open, her eyes widened, and she said, "How did you do that? It's gone, the pain is gone! How did you do that?"

"I didn't do nothing," I said, smiling at her. "*He* did it," I said as I pointed up.

Then she gave me my change, and as I was walking away, I could hear her talking to the people that had been standing behind me in line. "My tooth really doesn't hurt anymore! I can't believe it! Did you see that?" she said.

I've noticed that when my hands get real hot, if I can touch someone that doesn't feel well they start to feel better afterwards. Sometimes it lasts for a long time!

❊

A lady named Faye came to sit with me. She and her mother had driven many miles. She wore a pretty hat to cover her head—she had cranial cancer and had lost all her hair from chemotherapy). The doctors had drilled a hole in her upper forehead where they put the medicine inside. They had not given her very long to live. She wanted me to tell her what I thought.

I told her that I could see she would finish all the things that she had wanted to do for her children I saw special picture albums for each of the kids and special crocheted afghan with letters on it. "You will finish the afghan," I told her.

She lowered her head.

"You have a bad headache, don't you?" I asked.

"Yes, Karen, I do," she replied.

I then asked her, "Can I touch your head?"

"Yes, I don't mind at all," she said.

I laid my hands on her head and we prayed together for a long time. She said that it made her feel warm inside and that her body sort of tingled—and then the most wonderful thing happened: her headache went away, and it stayed gone for several days afterwards! Her Mother was very moved by it all.

Several days later, her sister called and told me all the things that Faye had been able to do over the days that followed, because she had no pain. She said that Faye was able to do many things that she hadn't been able to for some time. I was glad to hear that, and grateful that God had answered our prayers.

Then one day I got another call. Faye had finished all of her projects and she thought she would crochet an afghan for her child. She decided to print the name "Baby" on the afghan. It took her a while to finish it she would crochet in between naps. She finished the stitching on the name "Baby," and when the last letter was complete, she slipped into a coma and went Home peacefully.

❋

Teresa had crippling arthritis in both hands and had not been able to work in her garden for years. She had come to several of my earlier lectures. I had talked about the incident with the woman that had cranial cancer and how I felt the need to touch her head because her pain was so intense. After the lecture was over, Teresa had asked if I would touch her hands. We sat down to pray. We held each other's hands for some time. When we finished praying, tears were rolling down her face. I asked her if she could straighten out her hands and fingers and move them around. Amazingly enough she was able to move them much better. She came to see me many times over the next little while, and now she enjoys working in her garden again and has continued to do so since we prayed together.

✳

A young lady sat with me, she only wanted to ask me a few questions on this day. As we started, I began talking about some different things in her personal life.

"You want to ask me a question about someone with the initial 'T,' is that correct?" I asked.

"Yes, that's right, Karen, I do," she said. Then very somberly she asked, "Is Toni going to be all right?"

I hesitated for a moment, looking away from her. A young girl came to mind. "I believe the person that you are asking about . . . is on the other side. This is a girl though, not a boy, is that correct?"

"Yes," she answered.

"Well she is just fine," I told her. Suddenly I could see flames on top of my left arm and I began rubbing it. "There is a burn on this arm," I said as I rubbed the flames away on top of my arm. I watched the message play out in my mind, I tried to explain what I could see. "She is burned badly on her left arm, is that correct?"

"Yes that's right Karen, she said excitedly.

"I believe this is Toni's sister I'm talking about, though, Bobbie has the burn, not Toni is that correct?"

"Yes," she said smiling and looking up in the air as if she thought she might catch a glimpse of her daughter that was there talking to us (in spirit).

"There is a message for you," I told her. "'*Bobbie will be okay, Mom, her arm will get better,*'" the small spirit said. I could see where there had been many skin grafts, and more to come. Toni (the spirit) said, "'*It will take time, but it will all be okay.*'"

After it was over the lady told me that everything was correct. That she felt better knowing that her daughter was there and was able to communicate with her. She had never gone to anyone like myself before, so she wasn't sure what to expect.

I never second guess anything, whatever I see, I try to explain.

❊

The next woman walked in and sat down across from me. I still had a lot of stuff in my mind from the lady that was before her. I went ahead and asked her to be seated. "Just give me a few moments sugar," I said. "I seem to be having some cluster bumps going on inside of my head."

The lady chuckled as we tried to make small talk until the air cleared. "You take all the time you need to Karen," she said.

Things started clearing away and so I began to talk to the lady about what I could see. Suddenly the little spirit

(Toni), that had been with me before, was back again, and she said, "*Karen, This is my grandmother.*'"

I looked back at the lady a little surprised, I took in a big breath and said to myself, *Here we go.* "Okay the spirit I see in my mind is Toni, she says you are her grandmother. Does this make sense to you?"

"Yes," she said.

"I feel a man with me also. I think his name is Larry? The name starts with an L for sure. Does that make sense to you?" I said.

"Yes . . . I think so," she said. "He is showing me a Pontiac car, red and white interior, it looks like a Bonneville . . . I think. Does that make any sense to you?"

"Yes," she said.

"He says he is sorry. There is an uneasy felling of sadness with this person," I said. There is silence in the room. "Does this make sense to you?" I asked.

"Yes, I think so, Karen," she replied.

Now a female spirit shows up. "I get the feeling of the name Trudy. Does that mean anything to you?" I asked.

"The name does, but not the lady," she answered back.

"Humm, I'm confused slightly, I'm not getting anything else from this spirit," I said.

"Karen, there is someone that I want to contact if I could."

"Okay," I told her. Before I could say anything else, she gave me his full name. "Well let me see if I can locate him, okay?" A few moments passed by, then there was another fella in my mind's eye. I started to describe what he looked like. "Does that make sense to you?" I asked.

"Yes," she answered back. Tears began welling up in

her eyes and she leaned in closer, looking intently at me.

I started patting the top of my head! "This is some kind of message," I said as my hand continued to pat the top of my head. Then my hand moved over the top of my head several times! "Humm," I said, "What the heck is he trying to tell me here?" I thought to myself. "Flat Top," I said suddenly, "Oh my gosh, that's it! Flat Top this was his nick name! Your father called him that, is that correct?"

"Yes you're right," she said excitedly, "My dad did call him that! Oh my God, Karen you really are real!"

"Yes Ma'am," I said to her.

"Karen," she said and then paused, "I don't know the lady that you saw, but my name is Trudy.

"Well I'll be dipped," I said to her, smiling.

"I had wanted to make contact with Flat Top for years, Karen, but when you made contact with his brother first, that confirmed to me that you are not a fake." She was blushing.

I told her, "That's okay, I really do understand. That's why I always ask if what I see in my mind's eye makes any sense to you; that's what lets me know that I'm going in the right direction."

She had not asked any questions until after I started speaking with Larry. "Karen, when you told me about his brother, you downright gave me the heebie geebies. Larry was Flat Top's brother, he committed suicide years before Flat Top passed away," she told me.

"Oh . . . then that explains the apology we heard, huh?"

"Yes it does, Karen. The car you saw was a Pontiac Grand Prix, and it was red and white."

The Crash

THERE WAS A WOMAN NAMED MONICA THAT had come to see me. She is a successful owner of an insurance company. As I sat with her, she did not ask any questions, she just wanted to see what I could come up with. We had a very good visit. When we were done she was astonished at what she heard. The physical problems that she had endured were as I had seen them to be. She had never been as moved as this. Then she said, "How does this work with you Karen?"

"Well Monica, it's this way . . . if I want to help you my mind, um, well it just starts getting what it gets. Only you know how accurate I am, Monica, I don't! Oh, I have a pretty good idea of what I'm thinking and saying, but you alone know if I'm right or not," I explained. "If I am asked questions that are real and pertaining to your situation, the answers will come. But if someone tries to mislead me by asking something that is not relevant to their situation, it will backfire on them and they will get garbled-up goop (as I call it)."

She just laughed and asked, "Why would anyone want to do that Karen?"

"Some people just like to see me perform, if that makes any sense," I said. "I didn't think that would happen, but it has on many occasions. I just tell people to be as honest with me as I am with them and it (my gifts) will work right," I told her.

Well Monica and I hit it off from the get-go and our friendship grew over the next little while.

One day we went to brunch. When we arrived at the restaurant, I felt like I was in another world. This place was just beautiful. It had imported gates from France and exotic, wild animals on the land around the restaurant. As we drove into this wonderful place, I marveled at its beauty. There were white and colored peacocks roaming freely; one was even on the roof overlooking the verandah where we sat. I had never been to a place like this before.

As we were sitting there, I began to feel the presence of a man (spiritually) close to me. He was telling me that Monica needed to know that they were all okay, but that she needed to be made aware of what had happened. I began to listen as closely as I could, paying attention to what he was talking about. Then I conveyed this message to Monica, "He wants me to tell you about the heading they were on Monica, does that make sense to you?"

She looked shocked to hear what I was saying. Quickly she dug in her purse for a pen and paper. "Yes, yes, Karen it does make sense to me. Just a minute, let me get a pen and paper okay?" As she fumbled through her purse, she kept saying over and over, "Yes it makes sense, total sense! What is being told to you, Karen?" Before I could answer her, she said, "Who is this talking to you? Has he given you a name Karen?"

"I only get the sound of *pffft,* that's all Monica. I don't know if it's a name. There has been an accident in a helicopter, though. Three people have died in this crash Monica," I said.

"Oh my God, Karen, you are talking to the pilot," she said excitedly.

I continued on, "He is saying the very first thing he noticed was a smell . . . like melted plastic or rubber in the compartment. There was no smoke but the smell was there. Then he noticed that his gauges were not working right. He flicked his finger at the instruments on the panel in front of him. Then it started working again."

The pilot mentioned someone named Blake. He must have looked for this problem but found nothing. "I believe this was the mechanic," I said. It was as if I were able to see this happening from the outside of the helicopter—as if I were suspended in space above it, looking down. It looked like a twisted cinnamon roll at one point. As they were flying this was happening, he gave his heading at the time, and he called out numbers. He had switched the autopilot on and off, and then there was a bright flash. He said something about "microwaves" or "micro bursts." Then I could feel a rushing of wind that came from his right side.

Suddenly it was as if I was there, inside of the cockpit with them. I could see the wing window was to his right (that's where the wind was coming from) and the stick was in his hand; it was shaking very hard, almost uncontrollably. I could see the instrument panel in front of me. I was trying to explain to Monica what I could see at that moment.

Then I heard a loud bang or boom sound. I felt wind rushing from behind where the pilot sat and beyond where the nurses were sitting. I believe it came down the tail from where it was breaking up. The tail of the helicopter, where the driveline is, was breaking apart. The tail had hit the outside of the aircraft and caused a horrible cut in the skin of the helicopter. The gash was several inches long; it looked like a rip or tear in the long part of the helicopter on the outside. It looked like the tail had literally flexed itself around and bent sideways to do this. The tail blade had hit the driveline. It looked as if the driveline had been cut by the force of the tail rotor, and the whole tail was breaking away.

In the process of this happening, the brackets that held the top rotor began to feel the stress of the tail falling off. The top blades went sideways coming undone from the top where it belonged. The blades hit and cut the body of the helicopter as it also broke away from itself.

As I was describing what I was I was seeing, Monica was trying to write it all down. "Go on Karen, go on," she said.

"The three were thrown to the ground and died on impact," I said.

Monica asked, "Three, Karen, are you sure?"

"Two women one man," I replied. "The fire should not have happened. The tail fell several feet from where the main body of the helicopter wreckage was. Monica does this make any sense to you?" I asked her.

"Yes! Oh my God, yes, Karen, the accident wasn't even in this state. It happened last night, I was up most of the night on the telephone with the investigators," Monica said. She started to tell me about it and then she asked me if the man that was telling me this was still with us.

"Yes, I think so," I said.

"How is he doing this Karen?" she asked.

"I just hear his words that come in my mind. I just know, he said he was flying the helicopter," I told her.

"Oh my God, Karen, you had to be talking to the pilot," she said. Well, I just scratched the side of my head. "I sure hope so. I have never been inside of a helicopter before, but if this makes sense to you, then I'm happy," I told her.

"Karen do you think you could tell me what the helicopter looks like if I were to show you pictures?" she asked.

"Yes, I think so. I got a pretty good look at it, I think."

"What about the panel, Karen, could you describe what you saw more plainly?" she asked.

"I'll try to draw it for you, Monica, if that will help," I said.

"You couldn't have known about this, Karen! It just happened last night! The news hasn't even gotten hold of it yet," she told me.

I just shrugged my shoulders. "I don't know either, Hon," I said.

We tried to finish our brunch, but I could tell that she was absolutely taken by all that had been said. "Do you think you can talk to him again Karen?" I told her I'd try my best. She asked, "Why do you think he came to you here (at the restaurant) Karen?"

"Well Monica, it sounds like there are a lot of questions that need to be answered. I think he knows you're the lady that will be handling this matter, so I guess that's why, Hon." She asked me if we could get together again and talk about this further. I offered my assistance in any way that I could help. So we started to see each other regularly pertaining to this accident.

I had tried to describe the color, what the helicopter looked like inside, where certain medical instruments were, and other gadgets (as I called them) that were inside the helicopter. I had seen a few of the letters and numbers in my mind that day as well. This was all new to me. I tried to explain where all the equipment was and what it was used for. It was very compact for how much it had inside of it.

A few days later she brought me some flyers that had pictures of different helicopters on them. The helicopters were all different colors, but the pictures she brought were black and white. I looked at them and picked out the one I thought it looked like. She told me that I was absolutely right. There was a big investigation about this accident. The people that lost their lives were in the medical field. Although I never talked to any of the families, I knew of them on a personal level. I talked to all the individuals that were killed in the accident over the next few weeks. This was truly my turning point as an individual. I finally had accepted the fact that I could help after all. This was really different for me. I knew in my heart that I was helping to make some important changes in the structural particulars of this helicopter.

I was asked to fly to the state where this accident occurred, but I had to decline. The accident had taken place in a field. It covered a very large area and there was no way that I could physically walk out to the crash site, so I suggested the next best thing: I asked them if they could videotape the area and let me see it. I had tried to draw a diagram (on paper) of what I had seen in my mind before I viewed anything from them. I wanted to explain where I had seen everything first. I tried to be as descriptive as I could, even describing where they had found the people that perished in the crash.

I also drew a picture of the mechanical parts I had seen in my mind that I thought were faulty. That is when I got to speak to the aeronautical engineer. We first spoke over the phone, and he had said that he would get a video of the crash site for me to view. I knew that he had seen the drawings that I had put together for Monica.

At first there was a lot of speculation—I think it is hard for people to accept the kind of work that I can do, but I do understand. Monica had met with these people and they were stumped as to why and how this crash had happened. Monica persisted until they finally at least listened to all that had been told to me. This put a whole new light on their investigation; their perspective changed . . . but not easily.

The engineers told Monica that I most likely got all my information off the Internet. She explained that I didn't own a computer, that I was not computer literate, and that I had not even completed high school. I know that must have tightened their belts up. I never asked for one dollar for helping them out—I did it 'cause I thought it was the right thing to do and I didn't want to see this happen again. I wanted to help in whatever way I could.

I warned Monica that there would be other crashes that would be similar to this one, and the cause would be the same. I knew that parts of this helicopter needed to be replaced. Some parts had metal fatigue and some of the parts didn't have enough supports. I felt that they had made the tail longer a few years earlier by several inches. They also extended the tail rotor as well, also changing the type of blade. This was causing certain problems. The wiring harness was a complete disaster in my eyes. It was an accident waiting to happen. This is all what I tried to explain to the aeronautical engineer.

The aeronautical engineer invited me to his home to view the video of the crash. I could tell his wife was there as an observer. We started to view the video of the site and everything started coming back to me. I was there for many hours, and they took lots of notes. The engineer and Monica had received their reports on the accident several weeks later, so the particulars were in front of them, but not me. The manufacturers were trying to say the opposite of what I had seen. I disagreed with them, and I stuck to my beliefs.

It took almost two almost two years for the confirmation to come back to me. By the time the investigation was over, they had spent thousands and thousands of dollars. What I had seen was indeed what needed to be changed. I had been right from the start. The pilot had told me everything, so "he" was the one who was accurate . . . I just listened carefully.

I am so thankful that the changes were made. It will save many lives, and that is ultimately what we all wanted. Monica and her family went on vacation not long after it was all over—she had to get back to her normal life again. She said that she had heard my voice as clear as a bell when she was in the French Riviera. We had shared a short message that was sent telepathically between us, although she wasn't for sure if it was me she was hearing or just her imagination. She had most definitely heard me (as we found out later when we saw each other again). We had a great laugh on that one because we found out just how very real all this is for both of us.

When she came back to the states she called to see if we could visit soon. When she came she brought a computer with her and told me, "You need to write a book and tell about all these wonderful things that you have been blessed with Karen."

I started laughing and said, "Shoot-far kiddo, I can't spell or type."

She said, "Karen, the computer can do all of that for you, my dear. I think you can do anything you set your mind to Karen. I know God will help you. He always does."

Well, she was right about that. He has put many different experiences in my life, and I cannot deny these wonderful things that have continued to grow around me.

The Runaway

A WOMAN CAME TO SEE IF I COULD HELP FIND her daughter. She was almost sure she had run away. I only asked her how long she had been missing. She told me it was going on three weeks. At my request, she had brought a sweater that belonged to her daughter for me to hold so that I could sense her physical presence. In order to use my clairsentience, I need a personal item of the person that's missing.

As I began thinking about this thirteen-year old girl, I started sensing an image in my mind's eye. I described the girl to the woman.

"Yes, that sounds like my daughter," she answered.

I tried to study what was in my mind's eye for the next little while. I saw the young girl leaving in a white car. I told her Mom I felt as if the car was from out of state. California, I thought, but I wasn't for sure. Then I switched from one area in thought to another. I could see what appeared to be a road sign. It wasn't too clear. I could see lots of young kids hanging out on the corners and up and down the streets. I didn't like what I was seeing. This was not the way kids should be living, that was for sure.

I was seeing a white house that had many young girls living there. I started getting numbers in my mind's eye— the numbers were nine, three, and six. The house had a couple of steps going up to the front door. I felt like there was a window; I wasn't sure, but I seemed to be looking through it. I could see the young girl inside, her boyfriend was about twenty-seven years old.

I wasn't sure of how to explain this to the mother sitting there in front of me. The girl had run away because there was so much dysfunction in her home. I felt that the boyfriend had coaxed and lied to the young girl. I think he had lied to all the young girls. He told the runaway that if she could make enough money (prostituting) he would marry her. This young girl believed in him, but so did all the other girls that he lived with. He was using them all. I only told the lady part of what I could see until it could be checked out. I had seen a street sign, and thought maybe the numbers and the name went together, I wasn't sure. The woman took with her all the information that I had shared with her that day.

Not long after we had talked, she called me on the phone. They had found the girl in a place that was very similar to what I had seen in my mind's eye. The numbers were not in the sequence that I had seen in my mind, they were reversed. My guess is that I must have been looking at a reflection in the window. That was the only possible explanation I could come up with. What else could it have been?

I think one of the hardest things for me (emotionally) is to try to help mixed up kids. I have been fortunate to be able to right some wrongs with God's help. Many families have been able to get their lives back together and move on. It's hard for me to walk by a missing children's board. I don't mind telling people that I think they are worth it. We all need to hear that we are worth a great deal more than what we think . . . at least, that's my feeling!

If you can believe this, I had one person ask me if I thought I was handing out false hopes to families. "No," I answered her emphatically. I feel it is simply telling the truth, that's all. For some people, a hug is almost foreign to them unless there is a relationship or closeness of some kind . . . and that's sad. I like hugs and so do people. They never refuse one, and they always give one back.

Finding Peace

I T WAS IN THE EARLY SUMMER OF 1999 WHEN A young 19-year-old girl named Christie came to see me. When she walked into my house she commented on the peaceful feeling that she got. I told her that many people though the years had said the very same thing. "I feel it most of the time, myself," I said.

"It's very comforting isn't it Karen," she said.

"Yeah I think so," I said.

What a beautiful young girl, I thought when I saw her. She had scarf around her head where she had lost all of her hair. She had big round eyes and was a tall slender girl. When we first started talking, I told her how much the young man in her life loved her.

"Oh, really?" she said, "You can see him?"

"Well, I can *feel* him, if that makes any sense to you."

Her eyes just sparkled as she smiled from ear to ear. She wanted to know if he was going to give hr an engagement ring.

This was one time I wasn't holding nothing back, I told her everything that I could see. She was afraid he would reject her because of her cancer. "No way," I said, "He's here for the long haul, kiddo." I could feel a spirit had come in with her. I told her that I could feel someone in the room with us.

Her eyes widened, "Who is it Karen?"

"Well my first impression is a female . . . a sister . . . someone very close to you, Christie. She crossed over not long ago," I said.

Her eyes flooded with tears, but she had a smile on her face, "Yes, go on, Karen."

"Well," I said. "She is telling me for you to listen to your mom, does that make sense to you?"

She looked at me and kind of snickered, "Yes," she said.

Then I listened to the spirit, "Laura," I said. I was surprised, because I normally don't get names, just circumstances. "Hmm," I continued, "I believe Laura left this world from cancer as well."

"Yes that's right," she answered.

"However she was fighting a different type of brain cancer," I told her. We talked at great length about the other side. Christie told me she felt better after talking with her sister. She thanked me and I told her, "If you need me please give me a call."

Then very straight forward she said, "Karen, am I really going to die?"

"Honey . . . we all have to do that one . . . ya know. Think about all the good things that are gonna happen," I said.

"Good things?" Christie commented with a funny expression. "Karen they only gave me a little bit of time, I'm only nineteen," she said.

"Ah shoot, sugar," I said trying to sound a little more chipper. "They don't know everything, ya know what I mean, kiddo? Think about this; you were wanting to be engaged . . . right?"

"Yes," she said.

"Well then you better get ready, 'cause you got some plans to make."

"Oh do you think so, Karen?"

"I sure do! I'd bet you a dollar to a donut on that one. Shoot you gotta pick out your wedding dress, your rings . . ."

Then she got serious again and asked, "What about my time? Will I be gone in three to six months?"

"No," I said bluntly. "You're gonna see Christmas and you're gonna being in the year two thousand . . . and you're gonna see Valentine's Day."

She started grinning as she gave me a big hug. "I sure hope you're right, Karen."

"Hon, you can take this to the bank, and you won't hear me say that often," I reassured her.

"You aren't' afraid . . . . are you Karen?" she whispered in my ear as we were hugging.

"No," I told her, "There is a beautiful place in store for us . . . but that time isn't here yet. I'm more afraid of not living right than am of death, Christie, does that make sense to you?"

"Teach me Karen," she said, "If you can, please show me how to not be afraid." As she walked out that front door a big piece of my heart went with her. I'll never forget that child and the words we shared that day.

Not long after that Christie's mother Mary Ann came to see me and she brought me some homemade bread along with the best custard I had ever had in my life. This was my favorite dish. I felt like the luckiest woman to receive such a special gift. "If you only knew what my custard looked like! You could use it for brick mortar," I laughingly told her. Mary Ann told me that I had helped Christie out a lot. I didn't know what to say. "God makes it worthwhile for me to try."

Over the next few months, Christie and I talked. Her doctor had given her the new medicine we had talked about in our first meeting. It seemed to slow things down some. It was December and Christie her mother and another sister came to see me again. I couldn't believe this little girl's strength.

"I don't understand something Karen," she said. "I think I feel my sister Laura at times, like she is with me; is that normal?"

"You're asking *me* if this is *normal?*" I said, and we all kind of chuckled. "I think Laura is trying to make it easier for you. She doesn't want you to feel alone. Does that make sense to you?" I asked.

Christie asked if she was being punished for something that she had done. "No way, baby girl," I said "We lived in very fragile bodies, hon. Most of us don't realize how fragile our bodies can be until we have something like this to fight. Some of our bodies just have a deficiency; at least that is what I think. Sometimes we can fight it off and sometimes we can't but condemning you . . . no way sweetie; I don't think that Our God works like that at all. He loves us too much. He knew some of us were gonna have one heck of a learning down here, but this is the proving ground, ya know what I mean? With Him we have everything, without Him . . . I hate to think of that," I said.

"I hope you're right, Karen," she said.

"I know I am on this one, kiddo."

Then she asked me, "Karen when am I going to die?" the words came quickly.

"There will be an exchange, Christie, one will help the other; that's all I can see . . . nothing more," I told her. Christie was holding her sister Samantha's hand. "I'm sorry I don't know what else to say," I told her.

Christie said, "I think I understand, Karen, I think I do." So many changes, everything in her life seemed to be moving so fast. She just wanted it to slow it down. "Am I still going to see New Years Day Karen?" she asked.

"Yes," I said, "Nothing has changed at all, honey. You will see everything you and I have talked about, nothing has changed at all. Christie, your ring is on its way."

I wish so much that I could have changed things for her. It was so hard to see her hang on to every precious moment of life that was left. It had been a pretty emotional day for all of them, and the days that would follow. I cried that night for the sorrow that this family was feeling. I would have done anything to change the outcome of this one, but it was out of my hands. *Why did I have to say those words,* I thought. They hung in my ears for days after. "*There will be an exchange?*"

Then I found out she had received her ring and boy was she happy.

After Valentine's Day they had started giving Christie massive amounts of Therazin because her pain was so severe. Christie would leave her conscious state of being and go into the astral state of being with her sister. When she came in and out of her body, she told her mom what she was doing. Mary Ann had wondered if it was a dream, or if it was real.

"It is very real," I told her, "It is called a C.O.B.E., a *conscious out of body experience,*" I said as I tried to explain it.

Christie called me on the phone and told me how much she loved me. She told me she kept seeing Jesus standing in the corner of the room holding the hand of a little girl. "Are they waiting for me Karen?" she said with a very tired voice, "Can I go now?"

"Yes," I told her. "You let me know when you are ready to hear the audio tape, and I'll make it for you to listen to," I said gently. I was trying to make it easy for her, 'cause I couldn't be there. "Just give me a call when you are ready," I said.

"I'm ready," she said. "Then I'll make you a copy of the tape right now and I'll have it ready for your mom to pick up in a little while, okay," I told her.

"Thank you Karen, thank you" she said.

It was about nine thirty in the evening when Christie had called me. I hurried to prepare the tape. It wasn't very long until there was a knock on my door. It was Mary Ann, and I gave her the tape. Forty-eight hours after Mary Ann picked up the audio tape, Christie left this world. Her fight was done and she was at peace. The day this had happened, Samantha had been to her doctor; she was pregnant with her second child. This was the exchange that we were told about when we all sat together that day.

I was sitting in the front room after Christie's passing and then I saw her, just as pretty as a picture. She appeared with long blonde hair with little rose buds around her head and in her wedding dress. I could smell the roses. Christie just smiled at me and then disappeared. Mary Ann and her son came to see me later on in the day. I shared the picture in my mind with them; Mary Ann told me that was just how Christie had been during those sacred last moments with their family.

The memory will live with me forever . . . and so will Christie.

A Family's Message

IT WAS MOTHER'S DAY WEEKEND, AND MY FRIEND Kathy and I were getting ready to go out to lunch. I was getting my purse and oxygen tank when I felt a female spirit come close to me. I could hear her calling my name. I stopped what I was doing for a moment to listen.

"Karen," she said many times over and over. "Please, please, tell her."

I didn't know who this lady was, but she sure was trying hard to get my attention. Kathy had noticed that something was taking place with me; she can always tell when I'm being talked to.

"Are you all right Karen?" Kathy asked.

"Yeah." I think so," I said, "But this has a different urgency to it." Everyone that comes to me is important, but this; this was different somehow. "Something has happened, I just don't understand who this person is."

Again I heard, "Sara . . . please . . . tell Sara." I didn't know who she was referring to at all.

I told Kathy, "This lady wants me to tell someone named Sara that she is sorry, but I don't know anyone by that name, do you?"

"No, I don't think so," Kathy replied.

I just didn't know who she was talking about. I wasn't getting enough information to work with or understand, and at that point it felt completely hopeless. I just didn't know anyone by that name. Then a little bit more persistent the woman's thought came more clearly to me.

"Bob will take care of her," I heard her say, "Oh, Karen . . . tell Sara . . . it will be okay." There was a pause. Then just as clear as a bell I heard her say, "Angela dear . . . please tell Angela."

The name Angela stopped me in my tracks. Angela was Kathy's cousin. I didn't know her on a personal level, but she had just started cutting my hair. I heard these words, "Please let her know we are all right and that it will all work out. I'm sorry, I didn't mean for this to happen. Bob will take care of her."

I was dumbfounded and I wasn't sure what this message meant for Angela. Then just as quickly as she had come to me, the spirit was gone. I told Kathy all that I had heard. She looked puzzled and asked me what I thought was wrong.

"I don't know," I said, "But something bad has happened."

Kathy's face showed deep concern as she said, "Oh my . . . Angela . . . do you have any idea what it could be, Karen?"

"No, I didn't get all the message," I said. I knew that there was more to it, and within a few days it all made much more sense . . . sadly enough.

On Mother's Day, just north of Salt Lake City there had been a horrible car crash. Many people had lost their lives, including Angela's mother and father. Kathy called me on the phone and told me about the accident and that Angela's mother and father didn't make it. That's when I remembered what had happened the day Kathy and I were going to lunch, when I heard that lady talking to me.

The spirit that had talked to me had to have been Angela's mother, Kathy's aunt. Days later Kathy was told about the message that I had received. Angela called me and asked what I could remember about that day the spirit lady called out to me. I told her word for word what happened, to the best of my memory. She asked me if I would try to contact her parents. The services for her family were finished and the healing was in the process.

When Angela came to see me, we sat down and I began to talk, "I feel like your folks are here. They have been around you all, I can feel an awful lot of love and affection. I feel a lot of contentment here as well. They are so happy that the children are all being so thoughtful and conscious of each other's feelings. That is the most important thing for them. There is a man that I see in my mind. He is the father of the young man that died in the other car. In his heart he feels it was an accident. He knows this is not something that was purposely done. I see that he is trying to explain this to two women. One woman is intent on making the other female sue for money for the loss of the young man," I said trying to understand this tragedy.

I continued. "I feel a presence of spirit I believe it is female, I believe it's your mother, Angela. I can't see her, but I can feel her," I said. It was as if I could feel her hands on my shoulders patting them. "She has a message for you: '*it's okay sweetheart, it's okay. It's beautiful here on the other side. One of us could have stayed, I believe it was your father, but he chose not to stay.*' Your mother and father did everything together and they are still doing everything together. She was concerned about her little black sheep. I believe this was you, Angela, does this make sense to you?" I asked.

"Yes," she replied.

"But your mother doesn't mean anything derogatory by it."

I realized that this was the same woman that had tried to get my attention on Mother's Day. She had a severe pain in her chest, causing a terrible surge, causing her to stiffen her legs which caused her foot to floor board the gas pedal. Her arms stiffened at the wheel as well. I feel her heart was stopping in the process of the car accident. Her husband was sitting at her side, he knew something was wrong, and he tried grabbing the steering wheel. There was an incredible energy leaving her body. I call it 'the life force.' I see an officer sitting in his car not far from where the accident has happened. He saw it as it occurred. "'*Sara . . . tell Sara,*' does this make sense to you Angela?" I asked.

Her eyes widened with tears as she smiled slowly, drawing her hands up to her face in amazement. "What did you call me, Karen?" she asked.

"Sara," I answered back. "Does this make sense to you?" I asked.

"It most definitely does," she said. This was her temple name, a secret name that no one knew it except her mother.

I continued. "You've pondered and wondered if your religion was right for you. Your Mother says wherever you feel God to be is right for you, Angela. There is a difference in viewing life now."

"Your mother is still the beautiful woman that all of you remember, the higher spirituality of a consciousness that we on this level do not understand," I said. "Your mother has tried to touch you, to ease your heart, to give you contentment and assurance because all of this has made you feel as if you are in a void, in darkness. Your mother felt that you were separate from the others, Angela, and she was afraid for you in this life. Now she understands on a much deeper level," I told her. "God is found on a level that sometimes can't be seen by human sight. Most always it is within ourselves, and this is what she is trying to intensify for you because you have had so many mixed questions regarding religion, feelings, and family."

Angela's mother then gave me a memory of the two of them sitting at the dining room table when no one else was there. They had made a promise; one that was very profound. Her mother explained, *"Angela if I should die before you do, I promise to let you know somehow, some way, what it is like; and if you should leave before I do, make me that same promise."*

"Your mother is now keeping her promise to you Angela," I said. Angela's eyes widened with surprise as the tears were flowing steadily down her cheeks. "Does this make sense to you Angela?" I asked.

Nodding her head up and down and appearing slightly pale, she realized her mother was there with us in the room.

I continued, "Some of you feel that your father and mother could not possibly be able to console you in your time of need. But you need to know that they are trying to prove they are speaking to you now, this is not your imagination."

"Your parent's finances are going to be more at an even keel, but your brother needs to pay attention to a tan accordion folder because there are certain papers that are inside of it. I can see an accordion as well," I said. I was imitating a jester with my hands as though I was playing an accordion. "Do you know what I mean Angela? That's the only way I know how to describe what I'm seeing right now," I told her.

"Yes, Yes," she said. Angela's look was one of total amazement.

"It's kind of a tannish-brownish color," I said. "Your mother says don't worry about the house it's not going to be touched. The other family involved in the accident is not going to take it. They are going to settle with the insurance. Everything is going to be okay," I said, as I relayed the information. "I see a bunch of flowers; I think I am in your mother's backyard," I said as I described to Angela what the yard looks like.

"Yes that's correct Karen," she confirmed.

"Your mother has been blessed with such beautiful children," I said. I felt the need to blow Angela a kiss (something her mother always did).

"There are messages in the piano bench from your mother, Angela." Then another lady appeared in my mind. "This lady seems to be speaking another language. There is someone from the Gallup . . . White Sands, Mexico area. Hispanic, I believe."

"I think that's my grandmother who died six years ago," Angela said.

"I see a person that has lots of hair pulled back away from her face," I told her.

"Yes that's' right," she said.

"Angela, your mother says, '*Remember the garden?*' I believe there is a message in these words for you. This has been talked about in other circles, the ring of prayer, the garden means something for you. Conscious effort within one's self, it's so peaceful here."

"Your mother must have played the piano! The garden, the garden, your mother repeats herself. Your father is saying something about his accordion. He thinks it's wonderful that his Heavenly Father would allow such a meeting between two worlds.

"'*I could not let your mother leave without me, Angela. It was my choice, and you kids need to know this. It happened quickly, so fast that there was no pain for your mother, either, just a loud boom! You need to remember this,*'" Angela's father continued.

"'*Get as much rest as you can, because life will continue for you all in a good way. When the time comes, we will see each other again. Please keep your faith and keep it close to your heart; when the time comes, your mother promises to be here to help you along your path. I thank God for my existence here. I can only say thank you for sharing with me your most private life.*'"

The phone rang and broke the connection with Angela's mother and father. Originally, Angela's choice had been not to come and talk with me. She wasn't sure if she believed in this sort of thing. Now she had answers to her many questions. I had been able to explain, in-depth, her mother and father's feelings. Angela had received her father's musical accordion, and Nick had in his possession the accordion envelope that held the insurance papers that their dad had talked about. Angela also found a music book in her mother's piano bench. When she opened the book to the marker, the title of the song was "*In the Garden*," another answered question for Angela from her mother.

Now there had been no autopsy performed, so no one was aware of the physical condition that had been mentioned in the session. I ran into Angela at the grocery store some time after having sat with her. Her face was drawn from stress. "Karen," she said surprised to see me there, "They are going to exhume mother's body. Do you think they will find anything?"

"Yes," I think so I said. "They will discover she either had a stroke or heart attack while she was driving, as well as something wrong with her head. I'm sorry you all are having to go through this." Before I left, I told her, "It will be all right, I'm sure of it, hang in there, okay? I need to go, but I'll talk to you soon, take care."

A few weeks later Angela called me and told me that the doctors had confirmed that her mother had had a heart attack.

Several weeks later, Nick and I went to get our haircut. When we got there Angela asked if I would mind meeting her brother. I walked into the shop and there was this big, friendly man sitting there, his eyes just sparkled. As he stood up, he reached out to shake my hand. "I've wanted to meet you for some time, Karen; I hope you don't mind," he said.

"Heck no, sugar, not at all," I told him, "I appreciate being able to meet you as well. I hope I was able to help you all out."

He asked me if I would tell him the story while Angela cut my hair. When I finished with my story, he seemed to be moved by what he had heard. "How does this make you feel?" He asked.

"Well, sometimes I feel like I'm dreaming and other times I feel like I'm hiding under everybody's bed . . . if you know what I mean."

He just kind of laughed. "We are all so surprised at your gifts and so thankful that mother and dad found you," he said.

"You're welcome," I said as I stood up to let Nick take my place.

All at once I could smell wood burning. "Hmm, do ya' all smell that smoke?" I said as I sniffed the air.

Angela's brother could smell it as well. "Yes I do," he said.

Angela stopped in midair, her arms looked frozen as she smelled the aroma in the room. At that moment I felt Angela's father with us, saying, *"Turn the radio on,* In the Arms of an Angel, *Now!"* I told Angela, and she hurried and turned on her radio. The song started playing and we all listened intently to the words. It described to a tee what had happened to Angela's parents. The emotion was phenomenal. When the lady stopped singing, I could tell Angela was moved by it all and so was her brother.

I will never forget this family and the many messages that were sent to them. When I left Angela's that day, I went right to the music store and bought many tapes of that song. I took them back and gave them to Angela as a gift to her family. I read the lyrics to both the songs, *In the Garden* and *In the Arms of an Angel.* It is so amazing for me to read the messages that were there in black and white for this family. Both parents on different days had sent a message for the kids that they had left behind.

✳

"I have known Karen and her family for about 12 years; even before her almost fatal accident in 1994. I have known her throughout her many subsequent medical problems and other situations which brought her close to the veil. As a skeptical Police Investigator for Salt Lake County Sheriff's Office for many years, I have always found Karen's guidance and insight to be right on the money.

After I left the Sheriff's Office, Karen has continued to guide and direct my family and myself through troubled times with uncanny accuracy."

M.P., Salt Lake City, Utah

Visits From the Other Side

A Visit from the Other Side #1

We're all on a first-name basis when people come to see me. One afternoon two females came in to see me. They had said nothing about their purpose in coming to talk to me. One of the females was a thirteen year-old child, named Sandy. Margie, the woman that came with her, was in her mid-to-early thirties.

I began with Sandy. "I feel you have certain abilities that you haven't been able to understand yet." She giggled, pulling both of her feet up from the floor to put them in the chair where she was sitting, smiling from ear to ear but still not saying anything to me.

As she looked at Margie, our eyes met. "It's okay," I said, "I put my feet in the chairs all the time." I could feel her relax with my words as I continued to talk. Sandy had been seeing different things in her bedroom. At times she could hear talking. She thought they were in a tunnel. I told her. "The static electricity in your bedroom is high and your radio always turns itself off and on." She nodded her head in agreement.

"I told you so," she said to Margie.

Sandy had seen many things happen, but wasn't frightened. I tried to explain what I could see about her life and Margie's concerns were very obvious to me. Margie was not her mother, but a close friend. Sandy needed a place to stay because her home was dysfunctional. Her mother had signed Sandy's custody over to Margie.

Sandy had been telling Margie that ever since she had moved into her house this had been going on. As I continued to talk they both just said yes in agreement at all the phenomenon that was going on around them in this house. Margie asked if it would be possible to talk to Sandy's grandmother.

"We can sure try," I said and in a short time we were able to reach her. She spoke of the happiness that Sandy had brought to her when they lived together before her death. The grandmother mentioned many different memories that they enjoyed together. She used to love smelling the sheets after they had been hung out to dry on the clothes line all day, and when she cooked a bunch of apples that no one ate.

Sandy and the lady began to laugh because they remembered the day being mentioned. "That's right! Huh Margie," Sandy said. The grandmother also talked about her poor feet and the pain that used to be in both of her knees. Then the grandmother mentioned the blue metal container that had her favorite talcum powder in it. Sandy smiled real big and said, "Yes I still have it, as a keepsake." The grandmother mentioned that she was with two other family members on the other side. She was very proud of what Sandy was trying to do for herself, and to continue with the good friends that were helping her out.

Then I looked at Margie. "You have a question . . . about your mother?" I said.

"Yes," she said.

"Can you tell me about my mom?"

"Well," I said as I paused for a moment closing my eyes in thought. "I can feel a lady. I feel she has a deep pain in her left breast. It feels like there was cancer in this body.

Margie nodded, "Yes."

"There should be no more tears, because there is no more pain. Your mother is much better now. Does that make sense to you, Margie?"

"Yes . . . it does Karen," she said. "God bless you, and thank you."

"May he keep you in good health for many years to come," I told her.

❊

A Visit From the Other Side #2

As time went on, I became more and more involved in many people's lives. A friend of a friend would tell their friends, and people would find me somehow. Even the mail carrier somehow knew I was different. I very seldom left the house in the winter time because it's just too cold. It's hard for me to breathe when the weather is less than 32 degrees.

A little gal named Lucy came up to me one day. My mail carrier was a personal friend of hers, and she had told Lucy she thought I was psychic. I chuckled at that one. At any rate I went ahead and talked to Lucy and our friendship just grew. She started cleaning my house for me. She told me it bothered her to see me struggle so hard with my house cleaning. Lucy just started doing it, and it's been that way ever since.

Lucy is a pretty little Spanish woman with a faith that runs pretty deep. I had told her that I talked to spirit, although she had never been around me when spirit and I had talked, until today. Bless her heart. The first time it happened it scared the heck right out of her. she turned a little pale, made the sign of the cross and started praying to Baby Jesus as she fondly calls him.

"What's going on Karen? Talk to me, are you okay?" she said, "What do you hear?"

"Well," I said as I stuck a finger in my ear moving it back and forth, "There is a high pitch sound that comes from some of them before we talk, it's intense. It doesn't hurt, it just buzzes inside my head like bees doing the tango."

"What causes that Karen?" she asked.

"They do," I answered her.

"Ohhhh," she said. Her eyes were the size of fifty-cent pieces with the uncertainty of it all.

I sat quietly for a moment, trying to concentrate on spirit. Nothing. Absolutely nothing. "I think someone is trying to talk to me," I said.

"R-e-a-l-l-y," Lucy said still staring at me.

"I'm not for sure who it is though." I had told Lucy that the week before had been a real hair-raiser, as I called it. so I started telling her what had happened.

"It started out with a phone call one morning. I was in my bedroom getting ready for the day when the phone rang, it was Angie. I was standing in front of my dresser that has a mirror on it. *"Hello,"* I heard someone say. *"My friend is sick Karen, will my friend be okay?"* At that moment, I could see a woman's spirit standing in the mirror behind me. The reflection was of a thick woman with curly hair looking back at me. I told Angie, "She seems to be waiting for someone . . . David. Does that make any sense to you?"

"No," Angie answered.

I tried to explain to Angie that there was something else I couldn't put my finger on, something about "eighteen minutes," but I wasn't sure what that meant. Angie thanked me and that was the end of our conversation.

Lucy asked if I had ever met Angie's friend before. "No," I said.

"Did you know it was her in the mirror Karen?" Lucy asked.

"No I didn't," I said.

The phone rang again a short while later. Nick answered the phone. "Karen you need to take this call," he said. It was Angie. She told me her friend had passed away eighteen minutes after I had spoken to her.

Lucy rubbed her arms with her hands. "Oh man Karen," she said, "Doesn't that give you the goose bumps?"

"Well not really," I said, "I mean, I guess I'm starting to get used to it. I don't know how else to describe it. Then suddenly the lady that I was just talking about was there with Lucy and I.

Lucy sat there starting holes through me. "What's wrong Karen, what do you hear?" Lucy knew I could hear something she couldn't.

"The spirit is giving me a name . . . Geri. Oh, this is Angie's friend," I said.

I hadn't realized it but the name meant something to Lucy as well, there was no mistaking that. Lucy asked, "What is her name Karen?"

"Geri," I answered.

I'm glad Lucy was sitting down, 'cause I sure don't think her legs would have held her up at that moment.

"I must be crazy for talking to you like this," I said to her.

The look on her face said it all. "Geri," she replied. "Karen you said the name Geri right?"

"Oh Lucy." I said, "I'm sorry I shouldn't have said anything. It scares most people when I talk like this. I'm sorry honey, I wasn't thinking."

"That's okay, Karen," she said, "Can you still hear her?"

"Yes," I said. "What's she saying to you?"

"Well she says she sure liked her cokes and smokes, and she is kind of laughing, she must have had a husky voice," I told Lucy.

"Yeah . . . go on, what else is she saying, Karen?" Lucy had her hands on both cheeks, listening intently to every word.

"Geri must have been a clairvoyant or card reader," I said. I didn't know it but Lucy had been seeing Geri for over twelve years. Geri talked about readings that she gave to Lucy and some things that only the two of them would know. Geri also mentioned the two things that sat on her table when she would read cards—her smokes and and Indian figurine. People thought Geri spoke to it. Lucy used to laugh at Geri's refrigerator because there was nothing but Big Gulps inside.

Geri also mentioned her close friend, Patricia. Lucy didn't know who she was talking about. Geri said Patricia spoke at her memorial because they had been such close friends for many years. Geri had been known by many.

In one of Lucy's readings with Geri, months before she had died, she had mentioned to Lucy that she would meet a lady that would talk a lot. *This woman will help people along with spirit's help. This woman would be a friend to Lucy in many ways and many would seek her out for direction.* We guessed that had to be me. I came into Lucy's life because Geri was leaving this one. I had not previously known any of these people at all.

✳

A Visit from the Other Side #3

Jessica and Marcus came to see me one day. They both wanted to have a family so bad. The first time I had sat with Jessica, we just hit it off right away. Later she introduced me to her husband, Marcus. I sat with both of them alone and together many times. They had been coming to see me for over a year, and as our friendship grew so did my feelings for these two young people.

Jessica and Marcus had just recently bought a brand new home and they were trying to prepare to adopt a baby. At one visit, Marcus had come to see me alone. I told him that I felt that that he needed to get a flu shot. I could see some kind of trouble with sickness.

He looked at me, lifted his eye brows in a surprise and said, "Okay Karen I'll try to remember to do just that." Marcus worked as an orderly at a local hospital.

Later on, I went to visit my friend Kathy. She and I were sitting in the front room of her home. Kathy knew Jessica through work, and they were friends as well. All of a sudden, the light in the kitchen came on—the lights were those florescent tubes and it was incredibly bright, more than usual.

I glanced at Kathy and she said, "What the heck was that?"

"I think it's someone that wants to communicate with us, but they are having a heck of a time getting through," I told her. My impression was that it was a man. I began to feel real hot inside and then I felt like I wanted to cry. I had such mixed up emotions; something was sure taking place. I told Kathy, "This has to be someone I know because of the way that I feel." The feelings just started to well up inside of me. "Lord, help me to understand what is happening here," I thought to myself.

Then as quickly as it had started it stopped. I was taken off guard by it all, but then I just put it to rest and went on with my day.

The next morning I was sitting in the front room and a beautiful peace came over me; I could feel so much love. The phone rang, it was Kathy, she was told at work that Marcus had passed away over the weekend. We were shocked because he was so young and healthy. She said he had contracted a different kind of flu and it was a bad bug. It wouldn't have mattered even if he had been in the hospital, because this virus attacks the heart tissue, in three days it took his life. He passed away with his wife holing him in her arms at home in their bed.

My heart was so sad for Jessica and what she must be going through. It didn't take long for me to realize that Marcus was trying to contact me. Within hours after his passing Marcus had found me. At first I was unable to understand him, I believe it was my emotions that were holding me back.

Marcus told me that he had tried to tell Jessica he had made a big mistake and he was so sorry.

"What can I do to help you Marcus?" I asked.

He wanted me to tell Jessica that he had not changed his beneficiary card. He told the girl in the front office just a few days prior to change it, but the girl at the office wouldn't do anything about it because it was not her job. His ex-wife's name was still on the document and Jessica, his current wife wasn't. It was just an oversight, but it was a big one for Jessica. The timing was horrible. How could I tell this young woman that her husband forgot to change the beneficiary card? He got sick that weekend with the flu and passed away a few days later. Marcus was so sorry. He wanted me to explain to Jessica that he had just forgotten to take care of the card. Over and over he kept asking me to please tell her.

When I talked to Jessica, she sounded totally devastated. She was crying so hard. "Karen, why didn't you tell me this was going to happen?" she said.

"I didn't know he was leaving, sweetie; you've got to believe me, I had no idea. I just thought he was gonna get the flu, nothing more," I said. I was afraid she might have a nervous breakdown over it all.

I knew I had to let her know about the card but I didn't want to add more to her suffering. I couldn't tell this little gal more bad news. I had a hard time with the responsibility of this one, it was hitting too close to home. I begged God to make it clear to me how I could help.

Jessica had asked me to come to the viewing. I went a couple days later to the viewing to see Marcus. My friends Kathy and Joyce went with me. As we walked into the mortuary a little old lady (spirit) was drifting through the crowd looking at the people's faces. She was looking to see if she knew anyone. She went into a room that was across the way. There was also a man that walked by, and he nodded his head at me as if to say "hi" as he walked into the other room that was open at the end of the hallway. I had to sit down momentarily to get my senses together. The only other time that I had anything close to this situation was when my own mom had passed over. Kathy and Joyce asked me if I was all right. I just nodded yes. We walked into the other room where Marcus was. There were many gathered inside to bid him farewell.

Again I told him that I would tell her, but I had to have more time to work this out. Jessica was standing by Marcus' side. Her poor eyes were so swelled from crying and she appeared as though she were in a daze. I walked up to her and said, "I'll talk to you soon okay sugar? If you need me call me."

"Okay," she nodded. As we were leaving the building I had told the girls what had happened when we first got there.

Many days later I tried explaining to Jessica what Marcus had told me about the insurance papers. She was mortified. His ex-wife would eventually share the insurance money with Jessica, but it took many months before it all came to an end.

It has been some time now since this happened. Jessica gave me a little white angel that Marcus had given to her. I set it on the shelf along with all of my other figurines. The top of the angel bends back to make a small opening and handwritten note saying *God Bless you always* is inside. I still hear from Marcus once in a while, and we are still very good friends.

❋

A Visit from the Other Side #4

Two ladies came to see me, and as I met them in the front room they both seemed to be very nervous. They asked if it would be all right for them to record their session— they had brought their own tape recorder with them, and wanted to make sure they didn't miss anything. I felt that they needed to hear from someone on the other side very much.

I led them to a room where we could sit comfortably with each other. I got a feeling that by now I have grown very familiar with when spirits visit me. I relayed this to the ladies as I waited to hear the messages that were being sent. I hurried to get my own tape recorder on so that everything could be caught on tape.

I told them that I could sense four (spirits) people around me and one that was saying, "Mom" over and over many times to me. This lady (spirit) that came with them was the first contact. She wanted me to convey her feelings to them both. (Spirit) said she was really let down with the eldest child. The women just looked at each other, they had not asked any questions yet.

"Your Mom says that Dorothy, the eldest sister, has taken the wedding rings. You girls needed to know that your suspicions were correct. Does this make sense to the two of you?" I asked.

One of the ladies looked so surprised and raised her eye brows at me. "It most certainly does Karen," she said. Then the women looked at each other over all that was being said. The spirit was explaining to me that the ladies in the room with me were her daughters. They nodded back to me 'yes'.

"Mom (spirit) also says the family is wondering where her Cherry Wood jewelry box had gone. The box had been missing for some time."

"Yes, that's right, and no one said anything about it, not even the one who had taken is," one of the ladies commented.

"Mom (spirit) says that the oldest had taken it sometime earlier as well. She had tried to communicate with you but was unable to. "You had a dream," I said, as I pointed to one of the ladies.

"Yes," she answered.

"You were not sure f it was a dream or not, because it seemed to be so real to you," I said.

"Yes, that's right, Karen," she agreed.

"You girls need to know," I continued, "Your mom says it was easy for her to leave and go home with the others." Both of the ladies were nodding their heads, looking at one another in agreement and surprise. Still not one word had been asked by either of these two ladies so I continued, "Mom also says that you need to understand why her oldest daughter had done this. She was spoiled as a child and felt that this was the only way to keep a part of her mother close to her." I pointed to the other lady and said, "You are the youngest of the girls."

She simply nodded her head "yes."

I was viewing a paper with a title written at the top of it, the word 'Deed' was in my mind. The money had not been shared evenly and mom was remarking how sad this was for everyone. They were both just looking so surprised at each other and then back at me. "Yes," you are right about that they said.

Then another spirit came forward to talk. "There is a gentleman with the name of Oliver. Does this mean something to you?" I asked.

"Yes," they said. One of the ladies started to cry, but had a very happy smile behind the tears. "He is showing me a picture in my mind of two handsome young men, dressed in khaki uniforms. He's smiling at me and he is touching his head!" I told them.

He started rubbing his head and laughing all the while. When I connect with these (spirit) people, they often show me different things to do as I am sitting in front of their family and friends. He just kept on rubbing and laughing. "He said one time he had a full head of hair, only to lose most all of it later in life. Does this mean something to you?" I asked.

His wife was smiling from ear to ear. He told her how much he loved her and that she was so special to him.

He was so glad she changed her mind about leaving him. She had a sparkle in her eyes and she just shook her head yes. He remarked about how she had kept their marriage together for many years and how sorry he was for making her so miserable for such a long time. She told me she just wanted to go home so she could be with him. He told her it wasn't time yet, but that when it was her time he would be there for her—that he promised, and he never broke a promise.

❊

A Visit from Other Side #5

Dorothy was a very attractive woman that was going through a nasty divorce. It was in mid-September when she first started coming to see me. She was concerned whether or not her ex-husband was going to meet her halfway with support. We had a very in-depth conversation about her case. The ex-husband was from back East, and he had a lot of ties with unfavorable people. I could see he was hiding a lot from her, and I tried explaining some of these "missing pieces" as I called them—many of these things told her she would find with the help of a private investigator that she hired after her session with me.

I had also warned her that she would have something removed from her body. I didn't know for sure what it was, but I had held up my right hand and made a sign of a "C" with my fingers. I had asked her to have this checked out. I felt that it was urgent. I had told her this would be within a hundred and eighty days. She was in great health and found this to be somewhat puzzling. She had been under a great deal of stress over the divorce so she didn't take it all that serious.

At that time, I recall feeling there was an unpleasantness about this whole thing. I told her that I wasn't sure about what I was getting at the time, but I did tell her about the nasty taste I had in my mouth—it tasted something like burnt hair. It was real bad, and I knew it belonged to her. I also felt I was drinking something that tasted like metal. I have learned in the past that I have to tell people everything that I feel, because it means something to them.

I saw where there was going to be a hesitation of some kind in her divorce. Her attorney had told her that everything would go off as planned; I disagreed with him. The day after our session she called her attorney to see if anything had changed. His answer was the same, "We are headed to court. There hasn't been a change that I'm aware of."

Two months later she came to see me again. The same thing came up again in her session. She asked me if the divorce would be altered in any way. "Yes it will," I said, "But it will be okay." There was also something about her traveling to a warm place that appeared to be flat, although I couldn't tell where it was. She wondered if it could be California. "I guess it's possible, but I don't know," I said. She had made no plans to go anywhere.

Not much had changed since our first visit, but I tried, for her sake, to find anything new. I never know if there is going to be something different or not. For some people, things change in a matter of days; for others it stays the same for quite a while. I record all my words to them on tape so that they don't have to try to remember everything that is said to them. Once they walk out the door the lights go out as I call it.

Dorothy came back to see me in March. When she came in the door, she looked tired and it didn't take long for me to realize what had happened to her. I asked if she was all right.

She smiled faintly and said, "I am now, thanks to you and my girlfriend." We sat down and started to visit. A lot had taken place. She had shared the tape of her session with a friend. Her friend had got the impression that I was warning her over a health problem. Then her friend had asked her if she had gone in for her yearly mammogram.

"No," she said, "I had not." She hadn't noticed anything different; there was no lump that could be felt and there had been no tenderness. The friend talked her into going to see the doctor anyway, and it was a good thing. They took x-rays and found a tumor. The doctors wanted to operate as soon as possible. They told her she was very fortunate to only have that part of her breast removed. They sent her to Texas to have a treatment that was fairly new. Where they had sent her to be treated was very flat. They were successful in saving both her life and her breast. She had to cancel the court date because of the emergency surgery. She actually had her surgery one hundred and eighty days after seeing me last. She counted the days and told me.

Go figure! Most of the messages I get from the other side totally amaze me.

✳

A Visit from the Other Side #6

Janet was referred to me by a friend of mine that was in the same grievance group that she belonged to, although I was unaware at the time who it was. I have tried to help people in this situation before, and that is one of the reasons that she was told to come and sit with me. Janet had never been to a psychic before and she was a little bit skeptical at first, but most of my first-timers are. She had asked me nothing at all up to that point.

I have told many people that if I were in their chair I would feel the same way, so it really doesn't bother me to let them know that right off the get-go. I was just trying to explain how my gifts worked for and with people. I have found that I have my own signals that I use that might be different than others. Others that have similar gifts as mine work in different ways, I have been told. So I have found that we psychics are evidently different in some ways. I reckon we all have different strokes for different folks.

As I began to talk with Janet, I told her that I knew he was on the other side. Janet began to weep. Her eyes were a pretty blue, and when I looked inside them I could see much grief. I felt the need to explain a great deal to her as quickly as I could, because I knew that she had a message that needed to be given to her.

There had been a horrible car accident not to long ago, and it had taken her husband's life and changed hers forever. Her husband, whose name was Dennis, was trying his best to explain what had happened that terrible day. I saw an 18-wheeler heading straight for them. It had come charging across the median and hit them almost head-on.

The last thing Dennis said was, "Look at that, it's heading straight for us." They looked at each other and it hit them, ripping their vehicle in half. I believe Dennis died on impact, while Janet survived the accident. Everything happened so fast, that he didn't have time to tell her how much he loved her and that she made him happier than he had ever been. Dennis said at the time that he believed the driver had tried to do everything humanly possible to stop his rig, but was unable to. Dennis understood that the driver would have a very hard time accepting what had happened and would not be able to drive anymore after that.

Then he mentioned his daughter and he said he loved her very much. He also mentioned "the boys." I got the impression he was not talking about children though. I could see dogs and one of them had a hip problem. I asked Janet, "Does this make sense to you honey?"

"Yes," she replied.

"The dog is missing her master pretty bad," I told her. She just shook her head up and down. Dennis said that the dog would lay on the floor and put its head on its paws and just whimper. Dennis also implied that it wouldn't be long until one of his boys would be coming to him as well. The animal was in much grief, as well as in pain from old age and sore bones. Janet would take care of him until it was time to let him go, but that time wasn't now. Janet could not bear to lose any more of her loved ones, not after all she had been through.

At that point Janet replied that he was talking about their dogs and that Dennis had loved them very much and he did call them "the boys."

The settlement over the accident would carry on for some time before it would come to an end. Dennis mentioned that the fence needed mending and that the rain gutter on the corner of the house needed to be fixed as well. I told Janet I felt that a brother would help her with these things needing repair. She needed to sell the things that were in the garage from the body and fender repair work that he had done.

By this time Janet knew that we really had her husband there in the room with us. She asked Dennis if she should get rid of the veneer as well. "Yes," was his answer. He had used if for certain restoration in cars. Janet continues to see me to this day and we have grown very close as friends.

✷

A Visit from the Other Side #7

There was a lady named Sarah that came to see me that I had never met before. She wanted to get in touch with a relative that had crossed over to the other side. Sarah didn't tell me who it was that she wanted to contact, she just asked if I could see or feel anyone around her, and if I could, would I try to talk to them. I told her that I could feel someone the minute she had entered my room although I didn't know who it was yet.

As Sarah and I talked about what was said to her, "You have something new Sarah, a robe, pretty blue, pretty blue. I (spirit) have been trying to talk to you. Sarah will be able to straighten out the mess with the insurance company soon. I'm happy now, and I even got to see my sister that is here as well." Spirit was also telling me that Sarah's window was broken and it sure made a mess.

At that moment Sarah gasped and said that a big magpie had literally flown right into her window at her home, and had indeed made a terrible mess. Although the spirit didn't give me a name, Sarah had confirmed that her mother's sister had died and crossed over three years before. Sarah's mother had also died, so we discovered that it was Sarah's mother who was talking to us.

Sarah was so surprised at what she had heard and very happy that we had made contact with her mom. She had been having a problem with her mother's insurance for over a year, and for some reason the lamp in her bedroom kept burning the bulbs out. I told her that was her mother trying to contact her. Sarah also confirmed that she had indeed purchased a new robe, it was lying on her bed at home that very minute, and it was baby blue.

✳

A Visit from the Other Side #8

A lady named Kerri came to see me, and she seemed very nervous when she entered the room. I proceeded to tell her that everything would be okay, that I would not scare her or tell her anything negative, and that I wanted to help her in any way that I could. As I started to talk to her, two young boys in spirit form came to my mind.

Both boys were her deceased sons. One boy told me to tell her that he didn't want to leave his brother alone and that was why he had chosen to go too. Kerri started to cry. Her son tried to explain about an awful car accident that they had been in that took his brother's life right then and thereand had put him in ICU, where he died shortly thereafter, but their sister had made it through it all. Physically she would be okay, but she was having a hard time with the fact that she made it and her two brothers didn't. He mentioned how his mother, Kerri, had held his hand when he was in the bed in the ICU room where he heard Kerri telling him that he was going to make it.

"She really did see the light," he said, "Tell her it was not her imagination Karen."

As I listened to what her son was saying ,he said he heard his mom tell him how much she loved him and how she needed him to hang on.

He started to tell me about a poem or story that he and his dad had written together about skiing. I could see crossed skis sticking up in the snow. I told Kerri this, and she smiled. Both of her sons told her how much they loved and cared for her. Then one boy expressed that now he was helping other kids find their way home. He mentioned that there had been an avalanche in Switzerland and he wanted to help them out as much as he could, many had perished that day.

He asked Kerri why she was still hanging onto their clothes and he said he knew that she was going into their room to smell their clothes all the time. His father in the meantime was slipping further and further away from his mother and their marriage was in jeopardy.

I also saw that Kerri's husband was trying to go on with his life, and that he was trying to deal with the loss of his sons as good as he could. Kerri didn't want to forget them; she wasn't ready to let them go.

Her son mentioned the pictures she had of them on

the dresser mirror in her bedroom. Kerri confirmed this to be so. Her husband wanted her to take the pictures down, but Kerri refused to. They were not listening to each other at all. After some time, her husband began to grow more distant from her.They soon got a divorce; although I did not tell her at the time that divorce was in store for them.

She was happy to know that her boys could communicate with her. She mentioned after our session how much it had helped her. I felt sad for her loss. Later Karri gave me pictures of both her boys that I keep in my angel room with all the other pictures of family and friends that are on the other side.

❇

A Visit from the Other Side #9

Once a lady called me from Las Vegas, Nevada. She asked me for some numbers that she could use to gamble with I told her I didn't gamble. That didn't make a difference to her so I gave her these numbers: **12, 2, 60.**

She called me later and asked me to sit down. I asked her how much money she lost. She proceeded to tell me how the night had gone. She said at 12 midnight she had run out of money and needed to get some more, but there was no one close to her to help with change, and a cashier wasn't anywhere to be found. So she decided to walk away from the machine and get some more money.

When she did, a 60-year-old lady went up to the same machine and put $2 in the machine my lady friend was just playing on. The elderly lady won a great deal of money. I felt bad for her, but I tried to tell her that I didn't gamble. She laughed it off, but I felt that she was really sick about the whole thing!

❋

A Visit from Other Side #10

I was explaining to my daughter one day that I could get an impression off of different objects like keys or jewelry. One day Kim brought a necklace over for me to look at. When she handed it to me, I knew right away it didn't belong to her. I think she could see that I was sensing something.

"Do you get anything off of it, Mom?" she asked curiously.

I held it in my hand for a moment. I hesitated to say anything because I felt such sadness come over me. "Yes," I said, "Unfortunately, I do get something, Kim." I was reluctant to let her know what I felt.

"What do you get, Mom?" she asked.

"What I get isn't good, Hon: maybe we should put a tape in the recorder okay?" I said.

She looked at me with a puzzled look on her face and said, "Okay Mom, whatever you think."

As I held the necklace in my hand, I began to go deep into thought. I began to feel a troubled young man. He had a very dysfunctional life with drugs and paranoia. He had come to a point of suicide and was unable to stop himself from self-destruction. As I talked to Kim, I asked her if any of this made any sense to her at all.

She just stared at me with a pale face and a blank expression as she said, "Go on Mom, please."

I continued to let myself go deeper in thought. I wanted to talk directly with this young man if I could. A moment later I made contact with him. The message was this; "He is sorry. He had no idea that this would have such an impact on his family. He was not thinking of them; he was in his own world of pain at that moment. I believe it's his sister that he is sending this message to. Does this make any sense to you Kim?"

"Yes, Mom," she answered.

"Kim, I believe he was in great torment at the time and he chose suicide as a way out of his pain. I can see a rope hanging from the ceiling of his garage . . ." My voice trailed off because my vision was picking up the full picture of what happened. "This is where the family found him, Kim. Does any of this make sense to you, sugar?" I asked.

She nodded her head, yes.

"He sends his love to her (a sister I believe) along with caution to *'watch him.'*" I believe he was trying to prevent something like this from happening again, but in my mind's eye, it was too late. A cousin would follow in his footsteps within weeks.

When I was finished I handed the necklace back to Kim and said, "This is someone you know isn't it, Kim? A close friend to you, right?"

"Yes," she replied.

I handed her the audio tape of our conversation and asked her to give it to her friend. She was so amazed of what she had heard. This confirmed for my daughter that I indeed had the abilities that I professed to have.

Realizing My Gifts

(Calling it the way I see it)

In the beginning it was difficult to understand the things that were going on with me, but little by little I began to pay more attention to the deeper parts of my consciousness. This is how it works for me—I don't know if others are like me, or if I am like them. But this is what works in my mind.

I have never been diagnosed with any type of mental illness; however, my daughter thought I was a day late and dollar short after my accident, but that's as far as it went. I've had to search to find the correct names to explain what I live with 24-hours a day, 7-days a week. The way I see it, this is the best description I can give you.

Whenever I touch something, almost immediately I get pictures in my mind's eye. This is called **Psychometric**, which is a tool I use for some spirit communication. Not to speak to spirit, but to know of them and what they've done in their lives. The physical frequency and/or vibration I pick up from an individual's personal objects fill my mind. I see images of people, places, or events. I don't know how I am able to do this. I can smell odors that, on many occasions, no one else can. This is called **Clairvoyance**, which is derived from two French words; *clair* meaning "clear" and *voir* meaning "to see," But in my world, it's much more than that.

Clairsentience is neither actually seeing or hearing, but simply sensing. I have felt hot, cold, pain, loneliness, longing, joy, sadness, and despair without ever hearing a word. I have picked this up from people alive as well as deceased. I have the understanding that this is also called "**Mediumship**."

I receive audio as well as visual, which is called **Clairaudience**. I have gotten more comfortable in using this gift over time. When an article belongs to someone, they need to be the only one touching it. For me to be able to read the object clearly, it needs to have only their physical vibration so that I can sense it. It's like living in two different worlds at the same time.

I have not had much education to speak of and my vocabulary isn't large, but I try! I'll jump into the middle of most things if I think I can help. At times I am aware of physical ailments—I can feel people on a deeper level physically inside of my thoughts. I have on many occasions, been able to taste metal and burnt hair in my mouth only to find that the individual had cancer, or has had it previously. I've also seen gray splotches on the outside of their physical body, indicating to me that this is where the cancer is. So far I've had 27 accurate cases. I have been able to turn many sad days into brighter ones by finding the cancer early, sometimes before the person is aware they have it.

This was hard in the beginning because I try to stay out of negativity, as I call it. Some people call this "**Medical Clairvoyance,**" but I just call it "my stuff." I do not see myself as being a medical intuitive.

I've also been told that I am **Empathic.** Empathy is identification with an understanding of the thoughts or feelings of another.

I do not go into any type of trance. I only go into deep concentration. Sometimes I get symbol in my thoughts that help me to see what the individual is involved with. If I see **Eagles** in my mind's eye, normally the person in front of me has something to do with the government. There was once a man that came to see me dressed in old jeans, an oversized shirt, and tennis shoes. When he sat down in front of me I saw two eagles—one on each shoulder. Not only did I hear him, but I could also see him dressed in his black robe. I looked at him and simply asked, "Have you been a judge long your honor?"

He scratched his head, smiled at me, and shook his head in disbelief. He said, "You got that one right. You got any more like that?"

The only way I know how to describe spiritual healing is that when I touch someone and pray with them, an unusual energy exchange happens. A vibration comes from the right side of my body and from my right hand only. This administers a warm, tingling feeling that puts people at ease; and in many cases, has stopped their pain for as long as seven days. I feel in my heart that I do not have anything to do with this, except for issuing a prayer to our Creator and asking for their pain to be healed or taken away. I feel like a receptacle, but I have no other identification. Many have remarked that they can feel the sensation moving over their body as if they were being covered by a warm blanket.

✳

Symbols and Interpretations

Eagles: Normally symbolizes government. If I see two of them, it's usually a federal government worker.

Caduceus: if I see this symbol, it tells me they work in the medical field like a nurse, doctor, or medical assistant, etc.

Two Bands of Gold: If they are linked together, it means a strong marriage; if they are separate, it means the couple is having problems. If I see them interlinked and crack in one of the bands, he or she is having an affair.

Instruments Playing: They are either a musician or involved in the music industry.

Accepting the Challenge

WELL, MUCH HAS CHANGED IN MY LIFE AS YOU can see. I have thought on many occasions what would my life be like without my near death experience and the memories of the Guardian. He has given me a second chance to live and learn all the wonderful things that continue to happen around me, through me and inside of me. I will cherish Him always.

When I think back to some of the thoughts that we shared, the Guardian and I, when I had my near death experience, my heart swells with such love. I can tell you this, we have this right, this ability. But we have to take the responsibility to live it to the fullest. That's where my lesson has remained until this day. I guess it will until I go back home.

I can remember the pure telepathic mind exchange of thoughts that we shared while I was there. I was told that some people would think of me as being different, some would not accept me at all, some would think that I had fallen over the edge, and that some would not believe me. It would be hard for most people to accept this memory without the experience to back it up. It's my choice to shore it with you and hope that it does for you what it has done and continues to do for me.

Some have said I have amazing accuracy—others think I'm out to lunch and late for dinner, and that's okay, too! He knows my heart and that's what really matters. This isn't a proving ground for me, it's my second chance to live right and do what I can to change people's perception of the word and themselves; to look for the best *inside of themselves* where no one seems to want to look.

I remember being asked by the Guardian, "Will you take the challenge, this challenge for your life?"

"Yes," I answered, I didn't hesitate. I didn't fear *life*, I feared *not living it*. I feared not trying to change what I could, if I could, or to at least try. I felt that I could do anything that was in my power—or at least I thought so at the time when I was there. But I was in a different plane of existence there. I had forgotten that life in a physical body would be challenging. I had to live this way so I could learn how to love myself and let others love me as well. It wasn't even a thought that I had at the time when I was there. I wasn't afraid at all—I just wanted to please Him. This has all been a learning experience through His love and tolerance for me.

I remember so many things, and it seems to continue almost daily. I have not forgotten—nor do I think I ever will forget—how much He loved me in that time. I knew for the first time in my life what love really is and what life is all about. This is how we are supposed to feel when love is there inside of us. We are to share it continuously and grow from that without expectation, only to learn and know that this is why we are here and to create the most peaceful existence that we can.

I also remember the quote, *"Let he who is without sin cast the first stone."* We all have obstacles in our lives, and without them we would not learn; at least that's my perception. That is why we get to live this wondrous thing called life. We can create a wonderful place of peace, just as it is on the other side. This is the proving ground for us, right here on Earth.

It is the most precious thought that I have. I know He still resides inside of me; I feel him most of the time and the love that he shows me will always be here. I know that He is what keeps me ticking. He taught me how to share that love and how to apply it in my life here.

The keys are here inside of me, right where they were all along. I didn't have to die to receive them, we all received them when we accepted this thing called life. And how we love each other and treat each other and ourselves is part of the keys of love and life. The light is within all of us if we but simply look inside of our hearts. The Guardian told me that day to *look with my heart* instead of my eyes. The heart never lies, the eyes . . . well they only see what they want or need to. Kindness starts within oneself—not to be selfish, but to love and honor ourselves with pride.

As he loved us so shall we love, the lesson of life for me is still in the process and school isn't out yet. I stumble through it some days, praying to understand what it is that I'm supposed to learn or remember.

I have been asked, "Have you ever wanted to just do yourself in and go back home?"

"No," I replied, "I'm too busy learning how to live, I

already know how to die. I don't want to take any short cuts."

I want to try to experience everything that I can humanly do. He showed me things there that took a long time for me to understand here. He has placed many different things in front of me so that I could see the changes, and believe me, I have seen many in this short period of time. I tell people that I'm just as surprised as they are with what I seem to be able to do, and then I marvel at the moment in my heart. I was told that if I came back I would have the chance to change many things. I can't recall all that was shared with me, but I feel that He is guiding me daily still.

I am still human, and I've had my moments when I think of what I *can't* do. Then I think of the things that I *can* do, and it's a different world. I'm the one that chose this path. My physical inabilities were my choice as well. When I first came back, it was the hardest thing to get used to living this way. "Why me?" I constantly asked myself. Even though I tell myself that this is real, I still find myself giving a little pinch every once in a while, like maybe I'll wake up and all this stuff will have been a dream.

At the time all of this was a hard pill for me to swallow. "Why would I choose to live this way?" The first year was the hardest. I would catch myself wallowing in self pity, asking, "Why me? Why did I have to come back here this way with plastic oxygen hoses?" But then when I started to remember it was my choice, that was a pill of another color.

Oh, for the longest time I was angry with Him for

sending me back here. Then I started recalling many different things and it started to make sense. Why did I choose to come back? I didn't think I wanted to live a life in anger. Physical life is only slower, that's all. It's much different than it used to be that's for sure. But now I smell the flowers instead of running over them. I enjoy so many things that I wasn't even aware of before. I thank Him every day for this experience that we call life. I'm glad I got a second change to love and be loved.

Everything that I have learned there and here seems to be at a high speed. Some of it is unexplainable. I know where it comes from, and that's it. At times I feel like I'm one big receptacle or antenna with a direct link. I no longer feel the need to prove myself to anyone, I feel like I finally fit in. I don't have a worthiness issue any longer. I just know that I have experienced something much, much greater than what mortal man can think of or accept at times, and I do understand that. The veil is thicker than we think for some of us, and thin for others.

I realize now that I'm in a position to be of service to my fellow man and the positive influence that He has given me is to try to be helpful and maintain peace and happiness for everyone that comes my way. He really is more than just GOD!

As he said to me, "Look inside your heart; the answers lie within."

My Prayer To Him

by

Karen Baldwin

I see you in my memory
Standing there so patiently
Just waiting for a signal
In my time of need.

You wait without wonder
Hoping that I will find
The love that's here inside me
Growing from your heart to mine.

Will I share what you have shown me?
Have I learned or have I failed?
This path gets awfully tricky
Sometimes I lose my trail.

Can I carry what is needed?
Will I look to somehow find
This is only just my lesson
In this life that is called mine.

I know you've been there for me
And sometimes I did not hear
Your words of hope and wisdom
That you've sent throughout my years.

Your light has always warmed me
It has always been my guide
Where would I be without you
Standing by my side?

Thank you for my lessons
Thank you for my past
And thank you for proving to me
That real love always lasts.

You have taught me many lessons
From beginning to the end.
You have been there when I was lonely,
You have always been my friend.

In good times, you've brought me laughter.
In sad times, you brought me tears,
To wash away the sadness
That I've known throughout my years.

Have I loved the way I should have?
Or was there another way?
Have I touched their hearts with compassion?
Did I give them enough praise?

Will their memory of me last a while?
Or will it fade away?
If you can please answer,
Answer me today.

All the things I could ever want
You have offered me
From the smallest to the tallest
Everything I could see.

There have been so many pleasures
I can't count them one by one
You have given me so many things
Since my life begun.

Look behind me, I think not
For I truly love the change
This life is worth living
Even though there has been pain.

Many things I could not have felt
If it were another way
Thank you for the blessings
That continue day to day.

My understandings have been many
Now they are called my own
From you never judging
Simply loving is all I've known.

In quiet times I reminisce
On how it's going to be
When my journey here has ended
And you come to comfort me.

A Few Moments . . . With Him

by

Karen Baldwin

On March 17, 2001 at 8:30 p.m. I experienced another
Near Death Experience and I was able to spend a few
more moments . . . with Him

I felt you watching
And your touch
As you tried to comfort me.

There was no fear as you grew near
And your faces I could see.
To feel the comfort and the peace
As life interfaced with death
You gave me love and understanding
As I learned my new found quest.

Life in all its glory
As the people rushed around
Trying to save this precious life
That had already been found.

How can I ever thank you
For giving so much love to me?
In such a little while
So many trials and wonders did I see.

You never fail, you've taught me well
In such a small amount of time
The gratitude and the eagerness
That flows from your heart to mine.

Help me to help them
With words of praise
For loving me as they do I will never be the same.

Thank you God
For being you.

www.ingramcontent.com/pod-product-compliance
Lightning Source LLC
LaVergne TN
LVHW091215080426
835509LV00009B/1010